PRODUCTIVITY FOR LEADERS

A Practical Guide to Time Management
and Stress Reduction

On the 10th anniversary of inmarios.com,
this book sees the light of day.

To the leaders and companies that trusted me, thank you for
inspiring me. May these pages provide you with the tools to
achieve success in your projects and organizations.
Your trust has been my driving force.

.

© INMA RÍOS 2023
© Cover design: Imagina Designs
© Editing and layout: Revenga Ediciones
© Cover photo: Marian Venceslá

Registration number: 2308315196189
ISBN: 9798859812110

INDEX

01

WHY AM I WRITING

THIS BOOK?

Over the last ten years I have had the privilege of accompanying hundreds of managers in developing their leadership. I have worked with leaders of small, medium, and large companies from very different sectors (engineering, healthcare, finance, agri-food, textiles, pharmaceuticals, automotive, etc.) and with a wide variety of departments (HR, sales, logistics, finance, operations, production, IT, administration, etc.). I have found that absolutely all of them have one thing in common: a lack of time.

This is something I experienced first-hand myself, especially the first time I had a team. I was supply chain operations manager in the Netherlands for a large multinational. The position required me to lead a team, to deal with new responsibilities, to report to my boss or to take important decisions. All this in between endless meetings, avalanches of emails that I could barely read and manage, continuous interruptions and solving unforeseen problems. Living constantly with that feeling of not being in control of the situation.

All day long you're constantly putting out fires, exhausted and feeling like you are not making any progress.

I hear this every day when I talk to my clients. In fact, one of the most requested training sessions is my Productivity and Time Management workshop.

In my book *Keys to Successful Leadership,* I mentioned that the ability to optimize productivity is a crucial skill for any leader, but it is not the only one. We cannot demand high performance from our teams if we are not capable of being productive ourselves. Moreover, the higher our level of responsibility, the more important it becomes to manage our priorities and work efficiently.

In this book I will expand on what I covered in my second book and show you a collection of methodologies and tools that, while not miraculous, can help you take control of your time.

You will see that these are not sophisticated or complex techniques, as they are within the reach of any professional. It is not about making your day-to-day life more complicated, but about simplifying it.

These are strategies that anyone can incorporate into their routines, and they certainly make the difference between going in headfirst or being in control, which will translate into positive results. I am not just talking about increased productivity and professional success, but also the satisfaction of seeing that you are making progress, that your time is well spent and the impact this will have on your stress levels and, ultimately, on your physical and mental health.

Each and every one of the methodologies that I show you in this book I have practiced first-hand. Not only have I practiced them, but they have worked for me.

I must also tell you that I have modified many of them to adapt them to my tastes, my routines, and my way of working. You can also adapt them as you see fit, according to your tastes and needs.

In addition, you can also combine them as you prefer.

The important thing is not the tool, but the way you use it. A simple paper and pencil can work wonders for you if you use them well. I also know people who become obsessed with technology and the most sophisticated tools only to find that they are useless: they are still late everywhere and have a huge to-do list that they never complete.

I hope this book will be of value to you, and most importantly, that you will put its teachings into practice from day one.

Are you ready to get more out of your time? Let's go for it!

This book is the English version of the original book in Spanish "El Líder Productivo". Therefore, there are moments when references to situations in Spain are made. Two of my books are also mentioned ("Claves para Liderar con Éxito" y "Equipos Motivados, Equipos Productivos", which have not yet been published in English at the time of editing this book, although they will be in the near future.

02

I AM LEADING A TEAM... WHAT NOW?

THE NEW PRIORITIES OF A LEADER

Leading a team undoubtedly has a huge impact on our productivity. I experienced this first-hand. Like many of my clients, I also faced this dilemma: Do I focus on taking care of my team or on executing the tasks that need to be done?

This is often the case of very good professionals who, in reward for their work and merit, have been promoted and now manage a team.

This is often the case, but the fact that they are very good at their profession does not mean that they find it easy to manage people. Leading teams is a delicate and complicated task. In fact, it is a great challenge even for those who have experience in managing people.

Having a team in your charge requires a change of mindset when it comes to prioritizing.

These professionals go from being experts at what they do to not knowing how to do their new job, simply because they have not assimilated their transformation from task manager to people leader.

They tend to act by doing what they do best, i.e., performing tasks. So, they focus on habits and behaviours that have brought them success in previous experiences, because they think that this is how they can solve the situation.

WHAT IS THE RESULT OF ALL THIS?

What these professionals tend to do is to return to their comfort zone, i.e., instead of taking on their new role as team leader, they focus on the tasks. They do this mainly to save time, to avoid confrontation or because they think they know how to do it better. This is why it is so difficult for them to delegate. Remember that they are usually great professionals, experts in those tasks and very committed to their work, so they tend to take on the functions of their team, bearing the full weight of their execution.

As a result, their day-to-day becomes a hell full of stress, lack of time and excessive workload.

The key here is to distinguish which tasks can only be done by us and which tasks, even if we can do them very well (even better than our team), we need to delegate. We have to get those delegable tasks executed through our team. It is clear that at the beginning we will need to invest time in training someone to take charge of doing those activities. However, once the training is over, we will have developed our team and we will have more time to do what we really need to do.

WHY DO YOU LACK TIME WHEN YOU HAVE A TEAM?

One of the issues that my clients with teams in charge need to work on the most is time management. Have you ever had a situation where you have been doing things all day long and in the end you haven't achieved anything? Busy all day, but without achieving your objectives and, moreover, totally exhausted.

It is very often the case that when someone has a team in their care, they feel overwhelmed by the lack of time. Several factors contribute to this:

Managing a team is a very complex task and requires additional time and energy to assign tasks, follow up, give instructions, train them, communicate, listen, etc.

Continuous interruptions. When you manage a team, they often come into your office, whether to resolve a query, bring you a report, or ask for a holiday or a pay rise.They demand your attention, your energy and your time.

Lack of delegation. Often the fact that you know how to do a task makes you fall into the trap of doing it yourself instead of delegating it. You now manage a team: your mission is to get your team to take care of those tasks. This requires an initial investment of time, but if you choose the tasks to delegate to the right person, you will see a return on that investment.

Letting ourselves be hijacked by the urgent, ignoring the important. This happens very often, these interruptions, these urgencies distract us and do not allow us to focus on the long term. We put out fires and in the end, we lose our focus. This prevents us from being productive and ultimately we do not achieve the results that really matter.

The new responsibilities that come with promotion. Often your hierarchical position puts you in charge of new responsibilities, including leading a team; it is crucial to be aware that the way you prioritize your tasks will change.

Not knowing how to prioritize or optimize where to invest our time and effort. This is often a consequence of the previous point. As we have new responsibilities, it is sometimes difficult to prioritize them and, therefore, to assess when and how to manage each task.

On the one hand, leading a team means that there will be activities that you no longer have to do directly, but your team will have to do them and you will be responsible for their correct execution. This means that you have to rely on your team to optimize our productivity and to distinguish the tasks you need to focus on.

Basically what we would have to do is:
- Identify tasks that only we can carry out and make them our priority.
- Identify those tasks that our team can do and train them to do them autonomously.

LEADERSHIP DEVELOPMENT:
THE KEY TO THE PRODUCTIVE LEADER.

One of the keys to increasing your productivity as a leader is to understand that it is closely linked to the productivity of your team. In turn, the performance of your team will be totally related to your leadership style.

Yes, you read that right, effective leadership is one of the most important tools you have, to make your team perform at its best. When you lead a team, you must focus on creating a work environment that fosters collaboration, effective communication, as well as the motivation and commitment of your employees. In doing so, you will be laying the foundation for a highly productive team.

But how exactly can a productive team help you save time as a leader? The answer is simple: by having a highly effective team you can delegate tasks more productively and trust your team to carry them out in the most efficient way. You will be able to focus on the most important tasks, the ones that only you can do, rather than constantly worrying about supervising every member of the team.

So how can you increase the productivity of your team and improve your leadership at the same time? In my book *Motivated Teams, Productive Teams ("Equipos motivados, equipos productivos"* not yet available in English version) you will find guidelines and methodologies to achieve this. If you lead a team, this book will help you a lot in your day-to-day work.

Some key points:

1. **Clearly defined objectives:** Make sure your team understands what is expected of them and what the objectives to be achieved are. Set specific goals and ensure that each team member has a clear understanding of their role in the project.

2. **Communicate effectively and openly with your team:** Give good quality *feedback.* Listen to their ideas and concerns and provide constructive feedback. Encourage communication between team members as well, so they can solve problems together and work more effectively.

3. **Situational leadership:** There is no one-size-fits-all leadership style. Adapting your way of leading to each situation will optimize your team's motivation and performance.

4. **Delegate tasks effectively:** Make sure that each team member has the necessary skills and resources to carry out the task you have decided to delegate. In this way, you are not only saving time for yourself, but you are also allowing your team to develop and become increasingly autonomous.

5. **Recognize and celebrate your team's achievements.** Motivate them to keep working hard and improving their performance. A motivated and committed team is much more likely to be highly productive.

I believe it is essential that when a professional manages a team, he or she should be trained and coached to acquire Leadership and Team Management skills. This can undoubtedly make the difference between success and failure. Leading teams is a complex mission, too important to be left to chance. Being a good leader is something you learn and train.

As a team leader, you play a key role in creating a productive and effective work environment. By setting clear expectations, encouraging communication, delegating tasks effectively, and motivating and recognizing your team, you can help increase the productivity of your people and save time for yourself.

Remember that productivity is a continuous process and, as a leader, you are in the perfect position to lead the way to greater performance and success.

KEY POINTS:

- Time management is a critical challenge for team leaders.

- Managing a team involves complex tasks and frequent interruptions.

- Leaders must delegate, prioritize and optimize their time and effort.

- Evolving from being a task manager to a leader of people can be difficult and requires a change of mindset.

- Focusing on tasks instead of leading the team can lead to burnout and lower productivity.

- Becoming a productive leader involves developing healthy and motivating leadership. It will help empower your team and lead them to carry out tasks effectively.

03

THE MICROMANAGEMENT TRAP

Over the last 10 years accompanying managers and middle managers I have come across many cases where, paradoxically, they have fallen into the trap of micromanagement. I say trap because they practiced this style of leadership with the aim of increasing productivity and achieving better results, but the only thing they achieved was just the opposite. I explain it in more detail in this chapter.

WHAT IS MICROMANAGEMENT?

Micromanagement is an overly rigid team management style, that involves excessive supervision or control of the tasks given to employees.

Micromanagement usually has to do with the personality of the manager, although sometimes it can come from the culture of the company.

WHY DO WE DO IT?

The intention of those who do this is undoubtedly a good one. They want to have everything under control, to ensure that no mistakes are made, that productivity is enhanced, and that no detail escapes them.

In addition, there may be other reasons:

- Need for control
- Lack of confidence
- Perfectionism
- Not knowing how to let go
- Fear of error
- Attachment to certain tasks (having been engaged in them before promotion to manager)

THE PARADOX OF MICROMANAGEMENT

As we have said, the micromanager's intention is good, but paradoxically, what he usually does is the opposite of what he is trying to achieve.

Contrary to what the manager may think, micromanagement ends up damaging the productivity. It also creates a demotivating environment in your teams that negatively impacts the results you are looking for.

These undesirable effects occur not only among his people, but also on the manager himself and on the results of his team.

WHAT NEGATIVE EFFECTS DOES IT HAVE ON THE EMPLOYEE?

Sometimes the origin of micromanagement does not stem from a controlling manager, but is part of the culture of the company. Some organizations practice strict control of their workers, even though these practices are becoming obsolete with respect to new leadership trends.

In the face of micromanagement, those employees with the most potential will not stay with the company. This management style, in the long run, fosters a lack of initiative and a brain drain.

If a company wants to maintain a policy of micro- management, it must assume that high-potential employees with talent and initiative will not stay long. It can only count on employees with no initiative or creativity and who are totally dependent on the instructions they receive for the future.

In general, the effects of micromanagement on the workforce will result:

- Lack of motivation
- Lack of self-confidence
- Lack of initiative
- Lack of innovation
- Lack of creativity
- Fear of error
- High levels of stress
- Talent drain
- Demotivation

This style of management is certainly not good with experienced *senior* employees who are expected to take initiative and contribute their "know-how". Nor does it work with new generations, such as millennials, who need more participative and democratic styles of leadership, and who do not hesitate to leave the company if its culture does not suit them.

WHAT NEGATIVE EFFECTS DOES IT HAVE ON THE MANAGER?

Interestingly, the main "victim" of negative effects of micromanagement is the manager himself.

You become so attached to control and detail that your day-to-day life can become an exhausting hell due to lack of time. It is often materially impossible to accomplish all the details you would like to!

Moreover, this focus on detail not only penalizes productivity and efficiency due to lack of time but also causes the manager to lose the perspective and global vision necessary for effective management.

Because they want to control everything, their teams dare not do anything without first consulting with them, and this means that these managers have to continually respond to the interruptions generated by their people. This can consume much of their scarce time and generate high levels of stress, with a negative impact on productivity.

As a result, the micromanager may suffer:

- Exhaustion
- Lack of time
- Loss of perspective
- Not having a global vision
- High levels of stress (which are also contagious to their teams)
- Frustration (there comes a time when it is materially impossible to control everything at that level of detail).

- Low productivity
- Focusing on unimportant details, leaving unaddressed priority issues.

In conclusion, we could say that the manager who practices micromanagement can become his or her own worst enemy, as he or she could generate his or her own self-destruction as a leader. They become slaves to their own leadership style.

CAN IT EVER BE USEFUL?

Maybe in the early stages of a company or a team this style made sense, or even generated good results. Also on isolated, one-off occasions, such as in extremely dangerous, delicate, important or critical tasks.

It could also work with new employees, those who do not know how to do a given task of a certain complexity.

Or simply when our own team asks us to do so. That is why it is so important to listen and read the signals we are given.

In any case, these would be very *ad hoc* situations and should not be taken as the general trend.

HOW TO GET OUT OF MICROMANAGEMENT?

If you have identified yourself as a micromanager and you have realized that you want to stop doing it, I suggest you start changing the way you work with your team.

Where should we begin? It's crucial to clearly state what you want from them and allow flexibility in how they achieve it.

Here are some important guidelines:

Set clearly defined objectives following the SMART format (Specific, Measurable, Achievable, Relevant, Time-bound), and if you agree on them with your team, even better.

Have regular meetings to address any doubts and be accessible to your team in case they require your assistance.

Fluent communication to give and receive *feedback*.

Listen to your team, they will give you many clues on how to adapt your leadership style. They can also give you great ideas and will be motivated by your listening to their input.

Delegate, lean on your team. That will free up time and energy for other tasks and you will also help the development of your team.

Performance tracking and a good dashboard to monitor progress more efficiently. If done well, you can even get self-managing teams.

KEY POINTS:

- Micromanagement is an overly rigid and controlling management style that can have negative effects on both employees and managers.

- Although the micromanager's intention is usually good (to control errors, increase productivity, not to lose details), this style of leadership often damages the motivation, self- confidence, initiative and creativity of employees, as well as generating high levels of stress and talent drain.

- In turn, the micromanager often experiences burnout, loss of perspective, stress and low productivity, which can lead to self-destruction as a leader.

- It is important to move away from this style of leadership to more participatory and democratic ones.

- In short, micromanagement is a real trap: its intention is to improve productivity and in reality the opposite is achieved.

04

FROM STRATEGY TO IMPLEMENTATION:

CLEAR OBJECTIVES,

TANGIBLE RESULTS

The company's strategic plan is one of the main criteria to follow when setting our priorities, i.e., what is important, when managing our team, our tasks, and ultimately our time.

Therefore, all our actions and those of our team must point in the right direction, in line with the company's objectives and strategies. As leaders, we will be key players in getting the message from the top to the bottom of the chain. These strategies will be translated into concrete actions so that the company achieves the performance and productivity necessary to fulfil the strategic plan.

Some time ago, in one of my workshops, I asked the question: "Do you have clearly defined objectives?" The room was filled with the company's management team and its middle management, some of whom, with a slight and timid nod of the head, said that they were not so clear. The CEO, who was present, reacted with surprise and anger, since the very same week they had presented the strategic plan with a rich event.

We must realize that these strategic plans, which are the pillars supporting where the company wants to go, must be "translated" into concrete actions. This is precisely where many companies struggle.

It wouldn't be the first time that a manager gets frustrated with their team because they don't seem to know what they are supposed to do. Sometimes, we assume that by defining the strategic plan, everyone will be clear about what is expected of them, but this is not always the case.

The strategic plan is created at such a high level that it can be very abstract for the last link in the chain.

A warehouse operator may look at the strategic plan and not understand it, as it seems disconnected from their day-to-day work. To bridge this gap, involving middle management from the outset is crucial. This ensures that they grasp and internalize the company's mission, vision, and values at the highest level and can convey them to their teams in accessible language. In other words, they will specify the actions needed in different areas to achieve these goals.

Sometimes, managers have mentioned to me that their middle managers tend to focus too much on operational details, which hinders them from maintaining a broader perspective and comprehensive vision of the company's overall situation.

Middle management must be adaptable in their communication to be understood both by their superiors in management committees and strategic meetings, as well as by their employees, some of whom may have limited education. This is why their role is fundamental in any company and is not an easy one. Therefore, the development, education, and training of middle management in this aspect should not be underestimated.

HOW TO DO IT?

Executives and middle managers are the key players in transforming this strategy into concrete tasks with a well-defined action plan that their team can understand. It is essential that this action plan clearly identifies not only what will be done, but also when, how, where, and by whom. Additionally, every action plan needs to be regularly followed up to ensure progress or redefined when necessary.

Team leaders play a crucial role in "translating" this strategic plan into objectives and actions for their teams.

Working at the level of management teams and middle management is important to cultivate healthy and motivating leadership. It is crucial to train these managers in practical tools that significantly aid in managing their teams.

In hierarchical structures, the message often gets diluted as it cascades down the organizational chart. To mitigate this risk, promoting shared and transversal communication, emphasizing cooperation over competition, enables everyone to become a bearer and agent of change.

During my High-Performance Team Development workshops, I guide companies and their leaders in defining objectives collaboratively and assist them in creating the necessary action plans to achieve those goals alongside their colleagues. These workshops encourage active and dynamic participation, facilitating the translation of sometimes abstract strategic plans into concrete actions that everyone can understand.

Involving employees in this process significantly increases their understanding of the strategic plan, yielding enormous effects on results.

KEYS TO SETTING SUCCESSFUL GOALS

It is crucial to translate this strategic plan, which may initially appear abstract, into clearly defined objectives.

Moreover, setting goals and achieving them has a powerful motivational effect. Not only that, but it also triggers a snowball effect: when you achieve one goal, you generate energy and motivation to pursue the next one.

Let's explore the main keys to do it effectively.

Key 1: Set short-, medium-, and long-term goals. Aim to have at least one goal for each day, week, and month. Completing daily goals will lead to greater satisfaction, fulfilment, and happiness.

Key 2: Visualize your goals in detail. Program your "radar" (known as the Ascending Reticular Activation System or ARAS) to capture relevant information for achieving your goals. Just like when you buy a certain car and suddenly see it everywhere, focusing on something sharpens your awareness of related opportunities.

Key 3: Write down your objectives. Putting your goals on paper helps organize and internalize them. Written goals are 80% more likely to be achieved.

Key 4: Be specific. Define your desires in detail. Similar to programming your GPS for a trip, the more specific you are about your destination, the clearer your path becomes.

Key 5: Make it measurable. Quantify your progress and monitor your advancement toward your goal. Seeing your progress will keep you motivated.

Key 6: Ensure it is achievable. Set realistic goals within your capacity. If a goal seems daunting, break it down into sub-goals, making it manageable and empowering.

Key 7: Make it challenging. Balance achievability with a degree of challenge. A more challenging goal provides stronger motivation for accomplishment.

Key 8: Set a deadline. Define a time frame for your objectives. Having a deadline prevents indefinite delays and gives focus to your efforts.

Key 9: Ensure sustainability. Align your goals with your values and avoid conflicts with other important objectives or people. A goal that aligns with your principles will lead to genuine happiness upon achievement.

Key 10: Reward yourself. Every goal should have a purpose and reward. Identify the driving force behind your objectives and use it to stay motivated during challenging times.

The "what for" will serve as our driving force during weak moments and on days when we lack the strength to persevere. Having a purpose, a compelling reason, or a rewarding outcome tied to achieving our goal makes it significantly easier to stay motivated.

WHAT IS ARAS

The Ascending Reticular Activating System, also known as ARAS, is a network of neural structures present in the brainstem. Its main function is to regulate alertness and attention in the brain. It acts as a filter for sensory stimuli, selecting the most relevant information and sending it to higher regions of the brain for processing.

ARAS receives information from senses such as sight, hearing and touch, as well as internal signals from the body. For example, if you are in a noisy environment and someone mentions your name, ARAS will be activated to filter out the noise and direct your attention to that specific information.

In addition to its role in attention, ARAS is also involved in the regulation of the sleep-wake cycle and plays an important role in the generation of alertness and wakefulness.

In short, ARAS is a neural system that controls our attention and alertness, allowing us to focus on relevant stimuli and keep us awake and alert.

All these are the ingredients that a good objective must have in order to be formulated correctly. Have you already set your objectives?

KEY POINTS:

- The company's strategic plan is a key piece to take into account when prioritizing.

- It is essential to "translate" and ground the strategic plan into concrete actions.

- Training leaders to engage their teams is critical to the successful execution of the organization's strategy.

- Setting clearly defined objectives is crucial for the productivity of any professional, team and company.

- Objectives should be formulated in the SMARTER: format: specific, measurable, achievable, challenging, time-bound, environmentally friendly and rewarding.

05

THE FIRST STEP TOWARDS IMPROVEMENT:

TIME LOGGING

When we have a health problem, we usually undergo a series of tests to help diagnose the problem and decide how it should be treated. Just as we have a blood test, we can also diagnose of our productivity.

The equivalent of a blood test to make a clinical diagnosis would be the time logging.

We cannot improve if we do not know where we need to improve.

When I talk in my workshops about doing this exercise, many people look at me and say "What a nuisance, that's going to waste even more of my time". Just as we don't have our blood tests done every day, time logging is not something we have to do every day. Logging our activity for 3 - 5 days is enough to get relevant information.

In this chapter we are going to talk about the benefits of tracking your time use as a diagnostic to help you be more productive. If you are a manager or middle manager, you are probably used to being very busy and having many tasks and responsibilities. Sometimes it can be difficult to know exactly how you are using your time and whether you are really being productive. This is where keeping track of the way you use your time can be very useful.

Tracking your time use simply means keeping a detailed record of how or where you spend your time during a given period of time (maximum 5 days).

This can include work-related activities: meetings, phone calls, e-mails, etc. If you also want to make better use of time in your personal life, you can also do this with other personal matters such as going to the gym or watching TV.

After all, this exercise is for you, so it's up to you to decide how you want to do it.

HOW TO DO IT?

Try to choose between 3 and 5 days that are as similar as possible to your usual routine. That is, if something extraordinary happens, it is a holiday, you have an unexpected trip or special event, it would not be representative enough, and therefore would not provide us with the relevant information to draw conclusions.

The idea is:

- Gathering information
- To analyse it
- Drawing conclusions
- To make improvement action plan

The idea is that throughout the day you record what you are doing.

Ideally, you should register:

- Time
- Task description
- Estimated duration
- Real duration
- If it has taken longer than estimated, indicate what has happened: interruptions, problems, time bandits, estimation failures, etc.
- Indicate what you could do next time to improve it.

WHAT ARE THE BENEFITS OF LOGGING THE USE OF YOUR TIME?

The benefits of logging the use of your time are as follows:

1. Identify time bandits: Tracking your time use allows you to identify activities that consume your time but are not essential to your work. By recognizing these time bandits, you can take steps to avoid them and enhance your productivity.

2. Understanding time estimation: Time tracking helps you become aware of how well you estimate the time required for tasks. You can identify if you tend to underestimate or overestimate time, enabling more accurate planning.

3. Know your energy level: By monitoring your time use, you can determine your most productive hours and when concentration is more challenging. This knowledge allows you to schedule important tasks during peak productivity times.

4. Measure real task duration: Objectively tracking time helps you understand the actual time invested in tasks, avoiding the misconception that time has passed faster than expected.

5. Improve planning: Knowing precisely how long tasks take enables better daily and weekly planning, ensuring sufficient time for important responsibilities.

6. Identify behaviour patterns: Time logging can reveal unproductive behaviours such as difficulty in delegation, inability to say "no," procrastination, or lack of discipline.

KEY POINTS:

- Keeping a record of how you spend your time is a valuable tool to boost productivity.

- Identifying time bandits, prioritizing tasks, optimizing your time, and improving planning increase efficiency and goal achievement.

- Logging time for just 3-5 representative days of your routine is sufficient.

- It involves sampling, drawing conclusions, and creating an action plan for improvement.

06

TIME QUADRANTS

In my workshops on time management, one of the first concepts I present is Stephen Covey's "time quadrants," where tasks are classified based on their importance and urgency.

DO YOU KNOW THE DIFFERENCE BETWEEN URGENT AND IMPORTANT?

Many people often confuse the two, and I myself was unsure about the difference a few years ago. I used to think they were the same thing. But they are not.

Urgent tasks are those that require immediate attention and cannot be postponed. For example, a house on fire requires immediate action, regardless of its overall importance. To determine if a task is urgent, we simply ask ourselves, "Does this need to be done now?" (regardless of its significance or whether someone else can handle it). If the answer is "yes", the task is considered urgent. However, it is essential to be cautious because what is urgent often makes noise, demands attention, distracts us from what we are doing, and can even drag us down. It is crucial not to let ourselves be hijacked by the urgent unless it is also important.

On the other hand, what is **important** is determined by our objectives, what brings us closer to our goals, and what we want to achieve in our personal or professional life. To determine importance, we must have clearly defined our short, medium, and long-term goals. When facing a task, we ask ourselves, "Does doing this task bring me closer to my objectives?" If the answer is yes, then the task is considered important.

For example, as a leader:

- Anything that helps you achieve your company's strategic plan is important.
- Tasks that only you can handle and cannot be delegated to others also fall into this category.

Based on these two criteria, Covey classified tasks into four quadrants:

QUADRANT 1: URGENT AND IMPORTANT

That which cannot wait, and which is also crucial for you. This is the crisis quadrant (an important client with a problem, a project that is overdue, a fire in your house…). Any task in this quadrant has to be done by you and you have to do it now.

What effect does it have on your productivity? The result of this quadrant dominating your life is increased stress, anxiety, burnout. No human body can withstand this for very long. We have all had certain times, whether in our personal or professional lives, when we accumulate work peaks: a new job, a change of operating system in the company, a move, a newborn child, etc.

If such situations are limited in time, we will be overwhelmed for as long as it lasts, but there will come a time when everything returns to normal. What is very harmful is if this "crisis mode" becomes our daily routine. It will eventually take its toll, not only on our productivity but also on our health.

What do you have to do with this quadrant? Surely, when we have something that is urgent and important, we must deal with it as soon as possible. It cannot wait and the consequences of not doing so will be serious.

But we also have to try to reduce this quadrant as much as possible. How? Well, although there will be tasks in this quadrant that we cannot avoid, very often (more than you can imagine) they are things that could be avoided by dedicating time to quadrant 2.

QUADRANT 2: IMPORTANT AND NOT URGENT

It is that which is important, but not urgent (at least not yet). In other words, it can wait, but you must not let it go if you want to prosper. It is the leadership quadrant. The quadrant of personal development, planning, anticipation, proactivity, problem prevention, empowering your team, training your leadership, training yourself, taking care of yourself etc.

What effect does it have on your productivity? The result of working on this quadrant is success. It is taking control of your time and your productivity. The more time you spend in this quadrant the more control you will have over your productivity.

What do you need to do with this quadrant? When you are in front of something important, that you see that brings you closer to your goals, even if it is not yet urgent, you don't need to do it right now, but make sure you don't forget it. Put it in your calendar, set a deadline.

In fact, we may have tasks that are currently in quadrant 2 and that, if we do not act, may become tasks in quadrant 1. This is one of the reasons why the more we take care of this quadrant, the more quadrant 1 will be reduced. We could also describe this quadrant with the old and wise saying: "Don't put off until tomorrow what you can do today".

For example: Imagine that you do not take time to take care of yourself. You can be sure that, over time, health problems will arise and eventually become urgent and important (illness, hospitalization, etc.).

QUADRANT 3: URGENT AND NOT IMPORTANT

Has it ever happened to you that you've been putting out fires all day long? Those days when you end up totally exhausted and, what's worse, with the feeling that you haven't made any progress. Well, if this is your case, you are probably totally immersed in quadrant 3. At least a large number of my clients are between quadrant 1 and 3.

These tasks may be important to others, but not to you.
It may also be called the "illusion" quadrant. Why? Because it keeps you busy all day long doing numerous tasks, you create the illusion that you have done a lot, but at the end of the day you have not achieved your goals.

What effect does it have on your productivity? Well, you focus on the short term and lose focus; you lose sight of where you really want to go.

What do you have to do with this quadrant? This quadrant must be delegated or you must learn to say "no". In fact, many are those who have problems with this quadrant: they let themselves be hijacked by the urgent or take care of other people's priorities instead of taking care of their own; they also find it difficult to delegate tasks that are not crucial but steal their precious time.

QUADRANT 4: NOT IMPORTANT AND NOT URGENT

The most absolute waste of time we can have. For example, we decide to give ourselves a well-deserved half-hour break in front of the television, which in the end turns into hours of TV trash. Or maybe we start looking on the Internet for what we need for a specific topic and we are assaulted by ads(those ones that chase you until they get you) and you get sidetracked from what you wanted to do. Without realizing it, you have spent hours surfing the net.

What effect does it have on your productivity? Total failure. The less time you spend in this quadrant, the better.

What should we do with this quadrant? We must be disciplined enough to discard it. At least until we get our time and productivity under control.

Quadrant 2 is the key: The more time we spend in this quadrant, the more we reduce our quadrant 1, and the more we take control of our lives.

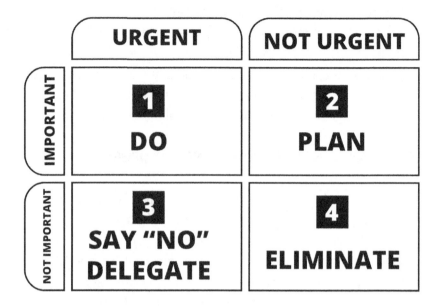

	URGENT	NOT URGENT
IMPORTANT	**1** **DO**	**2** **PLAN**
NOT IMPORTANT	**3** **SAY "NO"** **DELEGATE**	**4** **ELIMINATE**

It is true that there may be some tasks in quadrant 1 that we cannot avoid, but a large part can be eliminated. How? By working on our quadrant 2: planning, preventing, training, anticipating, taking care of ourselves.

And where do we find the time for quadrant 2? Precisely from quadrants 3 and 4, i.e. by delegating, learning to say "no", with more discipline and willpower.

Keeping these principles in mind when choosing our priorities is the basis for good time management, so that we can successfully achieve our goals.

Both in my time management workshops and in Leadership Development processes with my clients (individually or in teams) I include more tools and information on how to better manage our time and priorities. In my opinion (and from my own experience), the concept of time quadrants is a fundamental basis that, if well understood and applied, leads to excellent results.

Do you dare to apply it in your daily life?

WHERE DO WE OFTEN GO WRONG?

These are the most frequent failures in managing our productivity and, therefore, the ones we should avoid if we achieve the correct application of this concept of time quadrants:

Failure to distinguish between urgent and important can lead to prioritizing urgent tasks over important ones, which can have a negative impact in the long run. This mainly makes us fall prey to quadrant 3. Remember: the urgent often makes noise (notifications, calls, etc.) and has the enormous power to distract and even "hijack" us. Learn to differentiate between them.

Solving problems instead of preventing them can be a consequence of not differentiating between urgent and important, and can also lead to reactive rather than proactive management. Remember that if we apply well the concept of the time quadrants, we will be taking care of our quadrant 2, and this should not happen to us.

Failure to systematize important tasks can mean that time and energy are wasted in doing them in a disorganized way, which can result in reduced performance and efficiency. It can also mean that, if we have not set aside time in our schedule, day-to-day urgencies can distract us and those important tasks may not get tackled and remain undone. Remember: if you have an important task that is not yet urgent, give it the time it deserves in your planning. This is quadrant 2.

Not knowing or not wanting to say "no" can lead to work overload and lack of time for important tasks. This will cause you to fall into quadrant 3 again and again.

Not knowing or not wanting to delegate can mean that time and energy is wasted on tasks that could be done by other people, and this can lead to lower efficiency. Again, this is related to quadrant 3: urgent and unimportant.

Lack of discipline can land you in quadrant 4. It can be an obstacle to establishing and maintaining effective habits and practices, resulting in ineffective time management and lower overall productivity.

If you have made a record of your time, I invite you to analyse it and to ask yourself the following questions:

- Which quadrants predominate in your day-to-day life?
- How much time do you spend in quadrant 2?
- What are your most frequent failures?
- With what you have learned in this chapter, what could you do differently?

What you have seen in this chapter will not give you results overnight. But if you internalize it and apply it consistently, you will undoubtedly see that in the medium and long term you will take control of your time and avoid falling into these common pitfalls.

These concepts were a turning point in my time management. I often let myself be hijacked by the urgent without stopping to think about its importance, I found it difficult to say "no" and to delegate. My day-to-day life was immersed in quadrants 1 and 3, and little by little I began to dedicate less time to 3 and more time to 2. I encourage you to put it into practice today.

KEY POINTS:

- It is essential to distinguish between *urgent* and *important*.

- Quadrant 1: Urgent and important. You have to do it as soon as possible. Too much of this quadrant leads to burnout.

- Quadrant 2: Important, but not urgent. This is the key to success. Make room for it in your agenda.

- Quadrant 3: Urgent, but not important. It exhausts you and you lose your way. Delegate and learn to say "no".

- Quadrant 4: Neither urgent nor important. Discard it.

- The key is in quadrant 2: the more time you spend on it, the more control you have over your time.

07

DELEGATE

TO OPTIMIZE YOUR TIME

AND DEVELOP YOUR TEAM

If you are a leader, you know that your time is a valuable resource. And if you want to make the most of your time and that of your team, an essential skill to possess is the ability to delegate tasks appropriately.

If done well, delegating not only helps you reduce your workload, but can also be a great opportunity to develop your staff and make them feel valued in your team.

Delegation is not about passing the buck.

In fact, delegating would be the last phase of the application of the Situational Leadership methodology, if you are already familiar with this methodology, this chapter will serve as a reminder.

If you don't know it yet, I refer you to my book Motivated Teams, Productive Teams or to my online video-course "Leadership and

Management of High Performance Teams", where I explain step by step how to apply this method.

Delegation is something we should do gradually, so here are some guidelines on the different levels of delegation.

It is a matter of choosing the most appropriate level for each task, person and time.

LEVEL	Instructions	In what situation?
1	Look at the situation. Collect all the facts. I will tell you what to do.	The employee is new and you want to keep control.
2	Identify the problem. Propose alternatives with pros and cons. Recommend one for my approval.	The employee is being trained and you want to see how he/she deals with problems.
3	Look at the problem and tell me what you are going to do. Don't act until I authorize you.	You trust him but want to know what he does to avoid problems.
4	Solve the problem and then tell me how you did it.	Total confidence, you just need to know the final result.
5	Solve the problem. I don't need to be kept informed	Confidence so extreme that you don't need to know the outcome.

KEYS TO SUCCESSFUL DELEGATION

So how can you delegate effectively? Here are some of the main keys:

Determine which tasks to delegate: The first step in delegating tasks is to identify those that are not directly linked to your goals and can be done by someone else. Ask yourself: "Is this task something that only I can do?" If the answer is no, then you can probably delegate it to someone else.

Identify the right person: Once you have identified the tasks to delegate, you need to decide who the most appropriate person to delegate them to is. Think about the skills and knowledge needed to carry out the task successfully. Look for someone in your team who has the right skills and is interested in learning and growing.

Meet with the person and let them know that you trust them: Once you have identified the right person, it is important to let them know that you have full confidence in their ability to carry out the task. Talk to them and explain the task in detail, making sure they understand what is expected of them.

Train the person to do the task: It is important that you train the person to succeed in the task you are delegating. Give them the information and resources they need to do the task effectively.

Be accessible for support: It is likely that the person to whom you have delegated will need help or have questions as they do the task. Let him/her know that you are available to help and to support him/her in whatever you need.

Check the key points: The delegated task may have some steps that are particularly difficult or may be especially critical for successful completion. Be sure to indicate this at the outset.

Manage their performance: It is important to ensure that the person is meeting deadlines and expectations. Review their work and performance regularly.

Give feedback (both positive and constructive): Provide feedback to the person on their performance on the task at hand. If he/she is doing a good job, let him/her know and give recognition. If there are opportunities for improvement, provide constructive feedback and suggest how they can improve.

Encourage them to make progress: Whether you have had to correct a mistake or they are doing it perfectly, encourage them to keep going.

Acknowledge their achievements: When the person completes the task, be sure to acknowledge their work and thank them for their contribution to the team.

Delegating tasks may seem difficult at first, but by following these steps, you can do it effectively.

Remember that delegating is one of the keys to managing time quadrant 3 (urgent and unimportant). It is also a great way to encourage the development of your people and show your team that you trust them.

Let's get to work!

If you have done the activity log, go back through it and try to identify those tasks you have been doing that you could have delegated. Once you have identified them, try to determine who would be the most appropriate person and the level of delegation that best fits the situation. Design your action plan and do not forget to apply the steps we have seen in this chapter. Go for it!

KEY POINTS:

- Delegating can not only free up some of your time but can help the development of your team.

- Use the appropriate level of delegation.

- Make sure you follow the steps for a delegation effective.

- Delegating is a fundamental step in freeing yourself from the quadrant 3 (urgent and not important).

- You should learn the situational leadership methodology in order to be able to apply it more successfully.

08

LEARN TO SAY "NO"

Apart from delegating, learning to say "no" is one of the keys to keeping our quadrant 3 (urgent and not important) in check. This can be a big challenge, especially if we are concerned about maintaining the health of our personal relationships.

As leaders, we often find ourselves in situations where we are asked to do more than we can handle. If we say "yes" to everything, we run the risk of burning out and compromising our productivity.

Saying "NO" is not a bad thing but never saying it is.

It is important to think about how to say "no" in a way that works best for you. Here are some practical tips that can help you say it effectively:

Avoid giving a dry refusal. A simple flat "no" can generate discomfort, distance and resentment. Instead, try to explain the reason behind your refusal.

Differentiate between the person and the request. It is important that the person asking you for something does not feel that you are rejecting him or her. Make it clear that you are not rejecting the person, but simply that you cannot satisfy the request at that moment.

Give alternatives. Propose alternative solutions instead of simply saying "no". This makes the receiver feel understood and valued. A good alternative may even be better than the option initially proposed by our interlocutor.

Empathize with the other person. Give an explanation that brings you closer to the other person and makes them feel understood. For example, if you are asked to work overtime, but you prefer to spend time with your family, explain your situation.

Pay attention to tone. Use a tone that is both friendly and firm. Avoid being hostile or harsh. Remember that the way we communicate our refusals can have a big impact on our relationships with others.

Find balance. The key to healthy relationships (with ourselves and others) is balance. Do not commit to doing more than you can handle, but don't isolate or reject people either. Find the right team for you.

Remember: saying "no" is important for your well- being and productivity. Learn how to do it effectively and without compromising your interpersonal relationships.

KEY POINTS:

- Saying "no" is the key to not drowning in the quadrant 3.

- You can learn to say "no" assertively without damaging personal relationships.

- Show empathy, watch the tone and the way you say it.

- Giving alternatives is fundamental to saying "no". successfully.

09

PARETO PRINCIPLE

This principle is named after Vilfredo Pareto, an Italian economist who observed that 80% of wealth was owned by 20% of Italians, and which has underpinned much of microeconomic thinking.

What does this have to do with productivity?

When I was a student, I remember that whenever I had to prepare for an exam, I would focus more on those topics or sections that were more likely to appear (based on tests from previous years). I would study the whole syllabus, although I would prepare especially well for those questions. That worked for me year after year.

Without knowing it, I was applying the Pareto principle, which basically tells us to put more focus on what will give us more results.

Basically, this principle helps us to prioritize and invest energy in what will give us the most significant results.

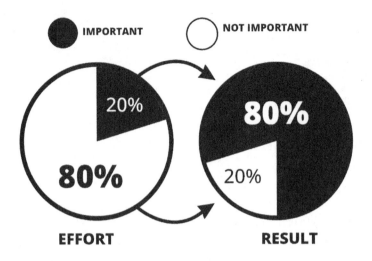

Find that 20% *of your tasks that generate* 80% *of your results!*

An example: This can even be applied in language learning. If we focus on the 20 % of vocabulary, verbs, grammatical rules, etc. that are used 80 % of the time, we will achieve an acceptable level of that language with much less effort.

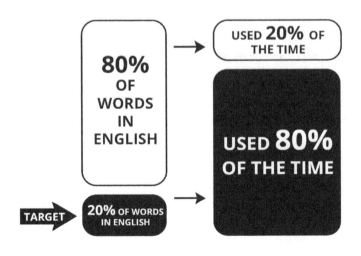

Application of the 80/20 principle in the company.

The business world as a whole seems to be consistent with the 80/20 principle, but its breakdown might be slightly different depending on the situation. These percentages may vary: 80/20, 75/25 or even 90/10. What really matters is to understand that a small percentage of your actions/causes (20 %) is responsible for most of your results/effects (80 %). Pareto theory is also very useful in business and organisational planning.

The Pareto 80/20 rule is commonly used in many ways in organisational and commercial management.

- 80 % of the company's profit comes from the 20 % of customers.
- The 80 % of the stock is made up of 20 % of the references.
- 80 % of the orders are concentrated on 20 % of the references.

It is useful in specialized quality management, such as Six Sigma, planning, decision making and general performance management.

Real examples:

Example 1: Cycle counting of stocks
One of the applications of this principle in my time as Supply Chain Operations Manager was in warehouse inventories, with a cyclical count of all references. Those items that accounted for 80 % of sales, the ones with the highest turnover (20 % of the items), were counted several times a year, while those items that had hardly any movement (80 % of the references) with an annual count was sufficient.

Stock Controllers were able to optimise inventory accuracy and their workload in the warehouse by focusing on what was really relevant.

Example 2: Complaint handling
With one of my clients who wanted to tackle the workload of the complaints handling department, we also used this principle. By analysing and focusing on the 20 % of the causes or problems that generated 80 % of the customer complaints. This made it much more efficient to tackle the situation, reduce the risk of complaints and optimize the resources of that department.

PARETO IN PROJECT MANAGEMENT

Pareto theory is also very useful in project management. How? For example:

If we take ten weeks to develop a project, and in only two weeks we can develop 80% of the functionalities, it would take eight weeks to develop the less crucial, but perhaps more difficult and complex 20%. In two weeks we could deliver a viable product much faster. The customer could even remove some less necessary, time-consuming and cost-intensive functionality.

PARETO IN TIME MANAGEMENT

The Pareto principle is extremely useful for bringing quick and easy clarity to complex situations and problems, especially when deciding where to focus effort and resources.

This same principle can be applied to your daily routine.

- 20 % of your effort can generate 80% of the results.
- 80 % of productivity loss is due to the 20 % of the cases.

So find that 20 % of your tasks that generate 80 % of your results with three steps:

1. Clearly identify your objectives and key activities to achieve your results, i.e. what is really important.
2. Apply the Pareto principle to prioritize your tasks.
3. Make sure you protect these key activities so that there aren't any deviations.

The objective here is:

- Those activities that provide you with the most relevant results and bring you closer to your goals should form your to-do list.
- Those activities that rob you of time, detract from your productivity or even have a negative impact should be on your "don't do" list.
- This means identifying which tasks can be delegated, automated or eliminated altogether.

KEY POINTS:

- Pareto is a good tool for prioritization.

- A large part of the results depends on a small number of shares.

- Identifying 20 % of the causes will help us to prioritizing our actions.

- Pareto is applicable to business, project and productivity management.

10

POMODORO METHOD

In this chapter I want to tell you about a time management technique that can help you to be more productive and efficient in your daily work: the Pomodoro technique.

If your biggest problem is interruptions, the Pomodoro Method can be your best ally.

The Pomodoro technique is a time management methodology developed by computer scientist Francesco Cirillo in the 1980s. The idea behind this technique is simple: work in short, focused blocks of time to maximize concentration and productivity.

The technique is called Pomodoro because Cirillo originally used a kitchen timer in the shape of a tomato (*pomodoro* in Italian) to measure the time blocks. However, the technique is very flexible and can be adjusted to suit individual tastes and needs.

This is how it works:

Choose a task you need to complete. It can be anything from answering emails to completing an important project.

Avoid any interruptions: Put your mobile on airplane mode, close the door, turn off all your notifications (*email*, WhatsApp, social networks, etc.), warn those around you not to disturb you.

Set a timer for 25 minutes or whatever time suits you best.

Work on your chosen **task for the** next 25 minutes without distractions or interruptions. If something distracts you, write it down in a list to deal with later.

When the timer goes off, stop and take a 5-minute **break.**

After the 5-minute **break**, start **another** Pomodoro **cycle** and repeat the process.

After four Pomodoro **cycles**, take a **longer break** of 15-30 minutes. This break will help you to recharge your energy and maintain your long-term concentration.

The Pomodoro technique can be especially useful for managers and middle managers who have a heavy workload and numerous interruptions in their day-to-day work. By dividing your work into focused blocks of time, you can maintain concentration and productivity, as well as reduce stress and mental fatigue.

When I explain this methodology in the classroom and tell them to put themselves in a "bubble" so as not to be interrupted, many counter that by saying that they cannot isolate themselves from the world.

It is important to understand that it is not about being in Pomodoro mode all day, but choosing moments of high concentration and productivity to activate it. And after that Pomodoro, or between several of them, resolve the issues that have arisen in those minutes of "isolation": checking emails, returning calls, etc.

What could happen that can't wait for 25 minutes? How long would it take you to complete that task using the Pomodoro technique? How much time/effort/stress are you adding to a task when you're experiencing continuous interruptions?

In addition, the Pomodoro technique also helps you to identify patterns in your work. If you find that certain tasks always take longer than expected, for example, you can adjust your expectations and schedule more time for those tasks in the future.

An example of Pomodoro adaptation:
How do I apply it to suit my tastes?

I told you at the beginning of this book that each technique can be customized to suit your tastes or working style.

In my case, when I have to do a task that requires more concentration than usual or that I need to complete as soon as possible, I activate Pomodoro mode.

To do this, I do the following:

1. I put my mobile phone on plane mode and also turn off my computer's Wi-Fi to make sure no distractions are coming in.

2. I close my office door and even put up a visible sign saying "Do not disturb" (sometimes I indicate a time when I will be available again).

3. I play music to help me concentrate. I usually use a Spotify playlist called *Deep Focus*.

4. The time I spend in Pomodoro mode depends on the task and my level of fatigue, I don't have a fixed time. Sometimes it just lasts as long as it takes me to do the task (sometimes up to 2 hours) and sometimes, if it is something more complex, I do several blocks of varying lengths until I complete the job.

POMODORO AS A TEAM

In the *in company* Productivity trainings that I give *it* is usually evident that most of the interruptions come from the colleagues themselves.

At the end of the workshop we usually leave a space for everyone to make a group action plan. They often propose to make Pomodoros and agree among themselves on the "rules of the game", for example:

How are they going to signal that someone is doing a Pomodoro (here I have seen proposals ranging from putting on headphones to putting a Post-it on top of the monitor visible to all).

Reasonable **maximum duration** of each Pomodoro.

Maximum number of Pomodoros per day.

What situations might interrupt a Pomodoro (agree on what would be considered a "crisis" or something of crucial importance)

In short, the Pomodoro technique is a practical, adaptable and effective tool to increase your productivity and reduce stress in your daily work. Try it for yourself and find out how it works for you - you can do it!

KEY POINTS:

- The Pomodoro technique is especially recommended to avoid interruptions and for activities that require a lot of concentration.

- This technique increases productivity and decreases stress.

- It consists of cycles of 25 minutes of work followed by 5 minutes of rest.

- After 4 cycles, a longer break of 15-30 minutes is taken.

- You can adjust it to your personal needs and preferences, modifying the length of the cycles and breaks according to what works best for you.

11

GTD METHODOLOGY

Getting Things Done or GTD is a productivity system created by David Allen, recognized worldwide as one of the most efficient methodologies for personal organization, as it increases productivity while reducing stress and anxiety levels.

GTD is based on the principle that a person needs to free his or her mind from unfinished tasks by keeping them in a specific place, so that he or she does not need to remember what needs to be done and can focus on getting the tasks done.

GTD in practice is applied in five steps:

Step 1 - Collect
It is the first step and consists of capturing 100 % of all your pending issues, projects and tasks that you want or have to take care of.

All of this is downloaded from your head and stored in your 'inboxes', which can be emails, mobile phone apps, tape recorders, notebooks, diaries, sticky note pads, etc.

Nowadays there are very sophisticated applications and software to manage tasks. In reality, it is not the tool but the use you make of it that really matters. A simple pen and paper can be very efficient if used well.

Step 2 - Clarifying
It consists of deciding what to do with each of the items you have collected in your inboxes.

Possible scenarios:
A) No action is required. There are three possibilities here:
1. **Discard it** completely.
2. **Incubate them** or save them for later.
3. **File them** as reference information.

B) It does require action. Then it will become a task and we will have different types:

1. **Project.** If the task is complex, we classify it as a project and break it down into sub-tasks that we will manage in due course.

2. **If it can be done in less than two minutes**, the action is done then and there. By doing this, the brain perceives that we are making progress and we will be able to reduce the feeling of anxiety and stress that overwhelms many people when they feel stuck.

3. **If it takes more than two minutes, we can opt to:**
   - **Delegate:** This is when a task needs to be referred to another person to carry out. The task will be placed on the **"waiting list"**.

- **Schedule**: Tasks that need to be done on a specific date are booked in our calendar or diary.
- **Defer:** Means to put that task on the *"to do list"*.

Step 3 - Organizing

GTD recommends keeping and organizing activities in lists. This way, a person can fully dedicate himself to the execution of a task and free his mind without forgetting the rest of the pending tasks that we will keep registered in these lists.

We can also manage to-do lists with applications such as Evernote, Trello, Google+ lists or Google Calendar. But you do not need technology; a pencil, paper and a calendar will suffice.

A list system to keep everything under control

One of the keys to this method is to create a system of lists that are reviewed on a regular basis. In this way, we can always keep everything under control in a systematic and efficient way.

These are the lists suggested by the method:

To do list. Having broken down the more complex actions or projects you have to do into simpler tasks, this list is where you will write down each of the next steps you have to do.

Projects. Allen points out that any task that requires more than one action or step is itself a project, which you have to annotate. The project should be placed on this list to be reviewed periodically. At each review, it is important to transfer to the *to-do list* the task or action that progresses the completion of each project.

On hold. This is the place for all the things that you have delegated or that a third party has to send to you to continue the completion of a task or project.

Someday. Here's everything you'd like to do someday but is not a priority.

Step 4 - Review
The lists that have been created should be reviewed periodically to decide what to do at any given time and to maintain control and reliability of our system.

- **Daily review:** We will review our *to do list* and our agenda or calendar.

- **Weekly review:** Calendar, our tracking file, our project list, someday/maybe, etc.

- **General review:** From time to time we will check that we are still aligned with our goals and vision, i.e. that we are still moving in the right direction.

Step 5 - Doing
At this stage you have to do the tasks and actions that are on your list at the time and with the tools you have at your disposal.

This is just a brief summary of GTD; in David Allen's book and on the Internet you can find very good resources and additional information.

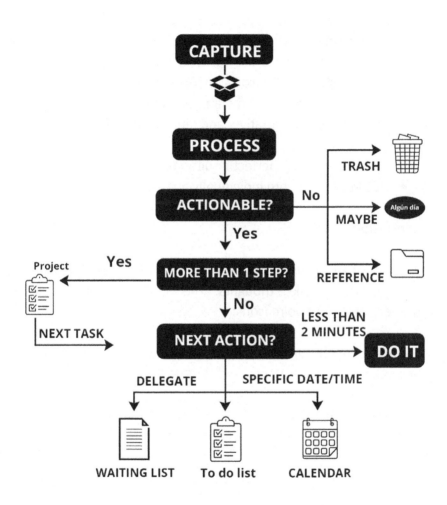

CAPTURE

PROCESS

ACTIONABLE? — No → TRASH

MAYBE — Algún día

REFERENCE

Yes

MORE THAN 1 STEP? — Yes → Project

No

NEXT TASK

NEXT ACTION? — LESS THAN 2 MINUTES → DO IT

DELEGATE — WAITING LIST

To do list

SPECIFIC DATE/TIME — CALENDAR

Trello and GTD

Trello is an ideal tool for implementing this methodology for several reasons:

- We can easily capture tasks at any time and place, as we can carry the app on our mobile phone.
- It allows us to capture tasks in different forms: emails, photos, files, social media posts, etc.
- Lists can be created and managed very easily.
- It is a simple, intuitive and affordable tool for everyone.
- Its free version is perfectly suited to start.
- It can be used both individually and as a team.

Conclusion

The aim of all this is to create a work routine to get all your worries, ideas, tasks, thoughts. This simple gesture helps tremendously for two reasons:

Reduces stress levels. Having something lingering in your mind not to forget it causes stress, and this method avoids it.

Increases productivity. GTD is a controlled system that ensures that our tasks are not forgotten and are executed.

In short, it is a system for peace of mind and the security that your tasks are under control.

KEY POINTS:

- GTD is a popular method of time management and productivity created by David Allen. It focuses on the idea that a mind free of worries and to-do's is more effective.

- GTD helps to set clear priorities and execute them effectively, reducing stress and increasing productivity.

- The five basic steps of GTD are: collect, clarify, organize, review and do.
    1. **Collecting** means capturing all tasks and commitments in one place.
    2. **Clarifying** involves reviewing tasks and determining their relevance and priority.
    3. **Organizing** involves categorizing tasks and projects for their implementation.
    4. **Review** involves setting goals and objectives clear and eliminate unnecessary tasks.
    5. **Doing** involves the execution of tasks according to their priority and urgency, as well as the regular review of the task list.

A system of lists is created and regularly reviewed and updated. Trello is a good support for this.

12

EMAIL MANAGEMENT

Effective email management is key to increasing productivity and reducing stress at work.

Email is an essential tool for work nowadays, personally it is one of my preferred means of communication. Because of my job, I have my phone on airplane mode during my trainings and meetings, and when I am finally available it is no longer time to call anyone or return calls.

But *email* can also be a source of distraction if we keep up with notifications. It can also be a source of stress when we see messages arriving faster than we can manage. Many of my clients really struggle with this issue.

Don't let your inbox be your control panel

The first thing to bear in mind is that we cannot leave control of our day in the hands of our inbox. Not everything that comes to us is the most important thing, and not everything that is most important comes to us by email.

Don't let your email inbox be your task manager.

That said, start applying it in this way:

Set specific times to check and respond to emails: I'm not telling you to ignore your emails, I'm suggesting that you choose when to check your *inbox*. Don't keep your inbox open all the time. Look at it as often as you want, make sure it doesn't pile up and that you manage it as often as your job demands, but don't let it be your task manager.

Turn off notifications: This avoids constant interruptions and allows you to concentrate on other important tasks. I also suggest that you turn off email notifications on your mobile phone to avoid unnecessary distractions.

Manage your mail

As mentioned above, not keeping your inbox open all the time does not mean that you are ignoring incoming mail. It simply means that we are the ones who choose when to check it.

That said, we can choose to check it as often as necessary so that our emails are answered promptly. In fact, people who know me, know that I respond to emails very quickly.

I don't have the tray open, nor do I have notifications, but I check it at the beginning of the day, at least every hour, except if my schedule of workshops and meetings prevents me from doing so. In those cases I check at every break in my training, after every training session, after every
meeting. My mail is always up to date.

Every time you check your mail, process it.

When you check your mail, try to process as much as possible, even if you are short on time. You may not be able to give an elaborate response to all of them, but at least you can manage what takes less time or is more relevant.

In fact, the GTD methodology can help you in this regard:

If action is required:

A) Answer:
- If you can answer it in less than 2 minutes, do it.

- If it requires a response, but requires a more elaborate response or is complex, you can even turn it into a task (and, for example, send it to Trello).

B) Delegate: Do it by adding the necessary instructions and keeping in mind that you will have to follow up (you can also leave it in your GTD "on hold" list). It is important to remember that when you delegate a task, you must make sure to follow up to ensure that it is being done effectively and within the established deadlines.

This involves reviewing the status of the task periodically and being available to answer any questions or concerns that arise in the process.

If no action is required:

A) File: If it is something you might need to refer to in the future or is information that you need to keep for whatever reason.

B) Delete: If it is of no use to you.

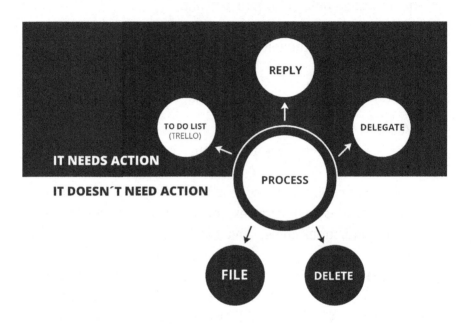

To the point

In addition, it is important to keep your emails short and to the point. This helps to avoid misunderstandings and reduces the time you spend writing and reading your *emails*. Try to be clear and concise in your messages, and avoid including irrelevant information.

Finally, I suggest that you establish a clear email policy for your team. Define when and how they should use email and set up a tracking system to ensure that important emails are responded to in a timely manner.

Out of office

When you are out of the office, it is important to set up an automatic message to let people know that you will not be available to answer e-mails.

In this regard, the "out of office" message should be clear and direct, and should indicate the length of time you will be absent, as well as the emergency contact person. This helps to reduce the number of unnecessary emails you receive while you are unavailable and prevents people from expecting an immediate response.

TIP: When you get back to the office, one tip that can help is to start reading emails from the most recent to the oldest. Otherwise you may be alarming yourself or solving problems that have already been solved. Believe me, it will not only save you time, you will also suffer less stress.

Some guidelines to follow

An effective way to turn emails into tasks is by using tools such as Trello or any other project management platform. By transferring the emails to a management tool, you can assign a due date and a responsible person, and to follow up on the progress of the task.

During holidays, set a clear and direct "out of office" message, and if possible, indicate who they could contact in your absence.

Using project management tools to convert emails into tasks is an effective way to maintain productivity and task tracking.

Remember to follow up on tasks delegated to third parties. You can use the GTD methodology.

Email management is not only a matter of organisation, but also of healthy work habits. It is important to set clear limits on checking and replying to emails, and to maintain a healthy work-life balance.

In this way, you can maintain efficient e-mail management and increase your productivity at work. Let's get to work!

KEY POINTS:

Mail is not your task manager.

- Choose when to check your email, with the frequency you believe necessary to keep it under control.

- Each time you review it, process it. Lean on the GTD methodology.

- Keep emails concise and clear.

- Turn off notifications to avoid distractions.

13

PROCRASTINATION

Have you ever left something for later because at that moment you didn't know where to start? Or have you thought that, as you don't have time to do it perfectly now, you'd better leave it for later? Does this ring a bell? Well, these are symptoms of procrastination.

This is something we have all experienced at one time or another.

Procrastinating consists of delaying activities or situations that should be attended to, substituting them for other more irrelevant or pleasant situations.

Procrastination is a common problem that affects many people in the world.

Procrastination is defined as the act of delaying or avoiding important and necessary tasks, replacing them with more irrelevant or pleasurable ones. Although we can all fall into procrastination from time to time, there are certain causes that can lead to this behaviour, and it is important to identify them in order to effectively address and overcome them.

WHAT ARE THE CAUSES? HOW CAN THEY BE OVERCOME?

Stress blockage:
One of the most common causes of procrastination is stress. When faced with a task that feels overwhelming or stressful, we may feel paralyzed and avoid it instead of tackling it. Change "I have to do it" to "I want to do it", this takes a lot of pressure off in case of blockage or fear of failure. The 10- minute rule, which I discuss below, can also help us in these cases.

Over-ambitious targets:
Sometimes the stress that causes us to procrastinate is because we have set such ambitious goals that they overwhelm us. In these cases, it is helpful to break the task into smaller, manageable chunks, what I call "slicing the elephant". When you "eat" the first slice, it gives you energy and motivation to get on with the next one. In this way, we can focus on one part at a time and move towards our goal without feeling so overwhelmed.

Fear of failure or success:
Another common cause of procrastination is the fear of failure or success. In both cases, fear can be so paralyzing that it prevents us from starting or continuing with a task. If fear of failure is what holds us back, we can remind ourselves that failure is a normal part of learning and is not the end of the world.

If, on the other hand, we are afraid of success, it is important to recognize that this does not have to be a problem and that we can learn to manage it with good emotional intelligence, assertiveness and knowing our limits.

Indecision:

Indecision can also lead to procrastination. If we have several options or tasks to choose from, we may feel overwhelmed and not know where to start. In these cases, it is useful to make a list of the options and evaluate the pros and cons of each one. Once we have a clear idea of what we want to do, we can make a decision and start working on it.

However, we must be careful not to fall into "paralysis by analysis". Sometimes it is not until we start a task that we know what the best option is, we have to allow ourselves to be flexible and change the plan if necessary.

Lack of knowledge:

Sometimes we procrastinate simply because we don't know how to do something. In these cases, we can seek information or training to help us acquire the knowledge we need to do the task.
We can ask others, take a course or search the internet for useful learning resources.

Perfectionism:

Perfectionism can also lead to procrastination. If we wait until we have the perfect conditions to do something perfectly, we may never get started. Instead of aiming for perfection, we can remind ourselves that the important thing is to do a good job, and that we can always improve later.

Remember, sometimes perfection is the enemy of good. Better done than perfect.

Awareness of the time available:
Finally, underestimating how long the task will take can also lead to procrastination. If we think we have plenty of time to do something, we may procrastinate. In these cases, it is important to set deadlines.

Lack of motivation:
If we don't feel like doing it, we can encourage ourselves in this way:

- Think of the reward, the relief we will be left with when we take that task off our *to do list*.
- Share it with others. When we commit in front of others to do something, we are much more likely to do it because of public pressure.
- The way we speak to ourselves plays an important role in motivation. Instead of "I have to do this", use "I want to do this".

THE 10-MINUTE RULE

If I had to recommend just one of the possible solutions for overcoming procrastination, I would go with the ten-minute rule. It is actually self-deception, but it works with spectacular results.

The ten-minute rule is to set yourself the goal of working on the task you are procrastinating on for just ten minutes. At first, this may not seem like a long time, but it is the minimum time to start the task and short enough so that you don't feel lazy to start and overcome initial resistance.

Once those ten minutes have passed, it is highly likely that you have engaged in the task and made much more progress than you initially thought. This is because the biggest obstacle for most people is not the work itself but rather getting started. Once you have begun, it becomes much easier to keep going.

In addition, the ten-minute rule is also effective because it allows you to approach the task in a more manageable and controlled way. By breaking the task into small blocks of time, rather than seeing it as a huge, overwhelming task, it allows you to focus on small accomplishments that move you closer to the end goal.

Another advantage of the ten-minute rule is that it is easy to implement. It does not require any special skills or additional tools, you just need a timer to make sure you work for at least ten minutes.

In short, the ten-minute rule is a simple but powerful technique to overcome procrastination. It is easy to implement and allows you to overcome the biggest obstacle: getting started.

I encourage you to try it the next time you struggle to start a task. You will find that you make progress and, more importantly, you will feel better about yourself when you complete it.

KEY POINTS:

- Procrastinating is delaying important activities by substituting them with irrelevant or enjoyable ones.

- The causes can be blockage, fear of failure, indecisiveness, lack of skill, perfectionism, overwhelming goals, or becoming overconfident with the time available.

- Solutions include changing mindset, training, reducing perfectionism, breaking the task into sub-tasks, applying the ten-minute rule, thinking about reward and sharing your purpose with others.

- The ten-minute rule is to work on the task for at least ten minutes to overcome initial resistance and focus on small accomplishments that bring you closer to the end goal. It is easy to implement and can produce spectacular results.

14

EFFECTIVE MEETINGS,

MEETINGS WITH ACTION

What are your meetings like, are they productive, or are they part of your time thieves?

After ten years working in Ireland and The Netherlands, when I returned to Spain I had to get used to a very different working culture. Well, one of the biggest differences I found was the management of meetings. I noticed that the vast majority of them started late, many were unprepared, everyone spoke at the same time, and worse, in the end little was learned. In my time management workshops, many people point out that one of the biggest "time bandits" are meetings, but how can we make a meeting really effective?

Nowadays many of our meetings are *online*, so the same principles we are going to see could be applied to our videoconferences. Below, I outline the steps to consider when convening a meeting, what you need to do.

This really makes the difference in making it productive and a good investment of our time.

STEP 1: PLANNING

The first step is to consider whether or not such a meeting is really necessary. Could it be solved by a phone call or an email? Or perhaps just by talking to the main actor?

Above all, avoid unnecessary meetings.

If we finally come to the conclusion that the best way to resolve this issue is to bring the key people together, we should be very clear about the answers to the following questions:

- **Objective:** What would the meeting be for?
- **Script:** What topics will be covered?
- **Participants:** Who will attend? Make sure that no one is absent or overbooked, otherwise the meeting will lose effectiveness.
- **Information:** What information is needed? If any reports need to be prepared, mail needs to be read, data needs to be collected etc.

STEP 2: BEFORE THE MEETING

Once all the above questions have been answered, the meeting should be convened. It is essential to communicate the details of the meeting to the stakeholders sufficiently in advance so that they can schedule it and organize to attend.

For this it is important:

Communicate to all stakeholders: date, time, place, agenda, duration and attendees.

Each and every one of the attendees should come to the meeting with their "homework done", i.e. they should have prepared everything that may be needed at the meeting: reports, prior reading of information, etc.

Here is an example of a call for a meeting by e-mail.

When it comes to video conferencing, this could be done from the same platform (Zoom, Teams, etc.) or the link could be shared via email (instead of the meeting room).

Dear Team,

We hope this message finds you well. We would like to invite you to an upcoming team meeting to discuss important matters and align our efforts. Please find the details below:

Attendees:
- John Smith (Team Lead)
- Jane Johnson (Marketing)
- Michael Williams (Finance)
- Sarah Davis (HR)
- Robert Miller (Design)
- Emily Wilson (Sales)

Date: September 15, 2023
Time: 2:00 PM (EST)
Location: Conference Room B

Total Duration: 1 hour

Agenda:
1. Opening remarks and welcome (5 minutes)
2. Project status update: Q3 goals and progress (15 minutes)
3. New marketing campaign proposal (20 minutes)
4. Employee feedback and engagement initiatives (10 minutes)
5. Team-building event planning (10 minutes)

Please come prepared with the information needed to discuss the agenda items and share your valuable insights.

We look forward to a productive meeting.

STEP 3: DURING THE MEETING

It is time for the meeting. Let's see what the keys to success are:

Moderator. It is useful for someone to act as a moderator of the meeting, either the organizer or someone else. This person will be responsible for making sure that all the following points are respected, that no digressions are made, that time is managed, that turns to speak are respected, that notes are taken and that the minutes of the meeting are taken.

Start on time. This is all a question of habits and company culture. If a company's employees get used to meetings starting a quarter of an hour late, they will always be late. However, if meetings start on time and are met with a closed door, they are more likely to improve their punctuality in the end. It is a matter of starting to do so.

In the case of video calls, we can help with timeliness by forwarding the meeting link an hour before the meeting so that participants receive a reminder and also have the link more readily available.

Focus on the agenda. Socializing is all very well, but it's best left to the coffee machine. It's about covering all the items on the agenda one by one, avoiding digressions with typical conversations about football, politics, etc.

When there is a clear script for the meeting, it is very much easier to stick to it.

Have you ever been stuck in a meeting where you know when it starts, but you don't know when it ends? In order for this not to happen, it is very important to respect the previous point, which helps you to see how much of the script you have left to cover in the time available. If we are running out of time, the script and the moderator will help us to get to the point.

Speaking time. This is probably another of the biggest differences between meetings in Spain and those in other countries. It is common for everyone to speak at the same time, to be interrupted or to form huddles and stop listening to the person who is speaking. So, it is important that this point is respected in order for the meeting to be productive.

Action plan. For such a meeting to do any good, it is important to be clear about what comes next, i.e., what to do, who should do it, when and how. A good action plan should be the outcome of any effective meeting.

STEP 4: AFTER THE MEETING

To put the finishing touches to the meeting and to ensure that it does not remain a handful of good ideas and intentions, it is important to do the following after the meeting:

Written minutes: This is the best way to formalize and ensure that everyone is clear about the conclusions and actions of that meeting, even those who couldn't attend! The key information will be summarized: attendees, discussion points, action plan, date of the next meeting, etc."

This meeting summary doesn't have to be a lengthy document. The idea is for the minutes to be something simple and practical, not a time-consuming burden for both the person writing it and the ones who must read it.

You don't need to invest a lot of time for the minutes to do their job. Simply by forwarding the call email and updating the information on who has attended or not, main actions and how the follow-up is going to be done is enough.

In the case of video conferences, the meeting could be recorded. so that anyone who needs it can see all the details on a delayed basis.

Of course, this is adaptable; a weekly operational meeting is not the same as a meeting to negotiate the sale and purchase agreement of a company.

Follow-up: We must follow up to check that the action plan is being carried out. Ideally, each individual should be responsible for informing the others when their action has been completed.

All these steps should be flexible and adjusted to different situations and different types of meetings.

In addition, we need to choose the type of meeting that best suits our needs, from Japanese-style meetings (standing up and lasting ten minutes) to meetings that may even last several days. Both the frequency and the format should be optimized to be productive and to fulfil their purpose.

It's all quite simple and, in reality, common sense, but well applied it makes the difference between a meeting that is a waste of time or something really productive.

What would you change about your last meeting? What will your next meeting be like?

HOW TO MODERATE A MEETING

To ensure that the meeting is productive and efficient,
it is important to follow some guidelines when moderating.
Let's get on with it!

Start on time: It is important that the meeting starts at the agreed time. To make sure that all participants are aware, we can send reminders the day before, and if it is online we can remember to link to the meeting one hour before.

Close the door: In the case of face-to-face meetings, make sure to close the door to minimize interruptions and distractions. This also helps everyone understand that the meeting has started.

Take a printed notice or a notebook with you: Have a notice with the agenda at hand to take notes, this can serve as the minutes of the meeting. It is also important to note who attends and who is absent for inclusion in the minutes.

The first 5 minutes: Instead of the traditional '5 minutes of courtesy,' I am in favour of starting on time, as a courtesy to those participants who have arrived punctually. During the first 5 minutes, let's make a brief introduction, reminding everyone of the agenda points and the duration of the meeting. This way, we make the most of the time, and those who arrive 5 minutes late won't miss key information.

Focus on the agenda: For the meeting to be productive, it is important to focus on the agenda. If someone wants to talk about something that is not on the agenda, let's write it down in the *Parking* (I will explain this later).

Speaking time: To ensure that all participants have a chance to speak, let's establish equal speaking time.

Remembering the time available: It is important to remind yourself regularly how much time is left to deal with the remaining agenda items. For example: "We have 30 minutes to deal with the 2 remaining agenda items".

Action plan: At the end of the meeting, agree on an action plan and how to follow up or the date of the next meeting.

Here are some tips on how to moderate a meeting effectively. Remember that the key is to stay focused on the agenda and be respectful of other participants' time.

PARKING: A USEFUL TOOL TO AVOID DIGRESSING

It is easy for other interesting topics to come up in a meeting, such as the *parking* is a good way of collecting these issues without putting the effectiveness of the meeting (i.e. that the entire agenda is covered and that it does not go beyond the planned duration).
For this we use the *PARKING*:

- *The parking* can be a blackboard, Post-it notes, or any other support to write down issues that are not on the agenda of the meeting, or that would take too much time to deal with during the meeting without making it too long.

- Ideas that are interesting or worth working on are noted down.

- These topics, if brief (5 or 10 minutes), could be discussed after the meeting (when the agenda for the meeting has been completed).

- If they are complex issues, they can be dealt with in a separate meeting, sometimes even more complex projects.

AGILE MINUTES:

What are agile minutes? It is one that:

- Can be done in a short time (less than 30 min).
- Sent within 24 hours after the end of the meeting.
- Can be read in a short time (less than 5 minutes).

What information should it have?

- Attendees and absentees
- Agenda items discussed
- Action plan (What, Who, When...)
- Follow-up
- Date of the next meeting

What to do if more information is needed?

Agile minutes are not intended to be a very detailed document of all the issues discussed, but a quick and agile guide that reflects the essence of the meeting.

Including all the details would make the minutes much more difficult to draft, take longer to draft, delay their dispatch and make it more difficult to find time to read them.

If any participant needs to go deeper into the topics covered there are different options:

- Participants can take their **own notes** at the meeting on the topics that impact them (not everyone has the same interest in all topics).

- Each team member can provide a **document with the most important details.**

- If a participant needs additional or more detailed information from that meeting, he/she can ask the **relevant person after the meeting.**

- In the case of online meetings, the meeting may be **recorded.**

How to make agile minutes in a practical way?

One of the best ways to make agile minutes is within the same email of the invitation:

Step 1: Print it out and bring it to the meeting (or on the computer/laptop).

Step 2: The main discussions under each agenda item are noted down.

Step 3: Once the meeting is over and with the freshest ideas, we update the email (with a different colour), which will then become our agile minutes.

Step 4: Sent to all invitees (participants and absentees).

Meeting Minutes and Action Plan

Date: September 15, 2023
Time: 2:00 PM - 3:00 PM
Location: Conference Room B

Present:
- John Smith (Team Lead)
- Jane Johnson (Marketing)
- Michael Williams (Finance)
- Sarah Davis (HR)
- Robert Miller (Design)

Absent:
- Emily Wilson (Sales)

Agenda:
1. Opening remarks and welcome
2. Project status update: Q3 goals and progress
   Action: Each team member will provide an update on their respective projects before end of the month.
3. New marketing campaign proposal
   Action Plan: Jane to refine the proposal based on feedback and share with the team by Friday.
4. Employee feedback and engagement initiatives
   Action Plan: Sarah to create a detailed plan for engagement initiatives and circulate it for review by next Wednesday.
5. Team-building event planning
   Action Plan: Robert to research and gather more information about the proposed team-building activities and present a finalized plan in the next meeting.

Next Meeting: October 2, 2023
Time: 2:00 PM - 3:00 PM
Location: Conference Room B

KEY POINTS:

The steps to effective meetings are:

- **PLANNING:** For what purpose? With what objective? What topics will be covered, who will be attending, what will be the theme of the event, and what will be the theme of the event? information is needed?

- **BEFORE THE MEETING:**
    - Notification: content, duration, attendees, place, date, time.
    - Preparing for the meeting: briefings, reading of pre-training.

- **DURING THE MEETING:**
    - Start on time
    - Focus on the agenda
    - Speaking time

- **AFTER THE MEETING:**
    - Written minutes: attendees, discussion, action plan, follow-up, date of next meeting.

- AGILE MINUTES: To reflect the most relevant issues in writing without taking too much time.

- *PARKING* is a methodology to avoid digressions without letting good contributions slip away, while the meeting focuses on the agenda.

- All these steps should be flexible and adjusted to different situations and different types of meetings.

15

AGILE METHODOLOGIES

Why do they arise?

Traditional project management has become obsolete in many cases, especially in:

- Projects in complex environments.
- Where early results are needed.
- Where requirements are changeable or ill-defined.
- Where innovation, competitiveness, flexibility and productivity are key.

In this chapter we are going to talk about two of the most popular agile methodologies: SCRUM and Kanban. Both are used in project and team management, and are very effective in problem solving and decision making in a business environment.

Each of these is discussed in more detail below.

SCRUM

One of the most popular and effective agile methodologies in project and team management. SCRUM is based on iteration and on collaboration between team members, and is divided into sprints (iterations) of a fixed duration, typically 2-4 weeks.

In SCRUM there are different roles and meetings that are fundamental for its correct implementation. Below I will explain each of them:

ROLES IN SCRUM:

Product Owner: The person responsible for defining and prioritizing the functionalities of the product or project. He/she is in charge of maximizing the value of the work carried out by the team and establishing the priorities in each sprint.

Scrum Master: This is the leader of the SCRUM team. His/her main objective is to ensure that SCRUM processes and practices are followed effectively and that the team is aligned with the project objectives. He/she is also responsible for facilitating SCRUM meetings and ensuring that the team has the necessary tools and resources to carry out its work.

Development team: These are the members in charge of carrying out the work and meeting the objectives established in each sprint. The development team is self-organized and multidisciplinary, and works collaboratively to achieve the objectives.

SCRUM

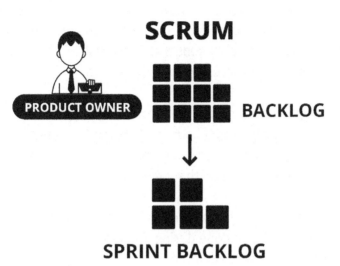

PRODUCT OWNER

BACKLOG

SPRINT BACKLOG

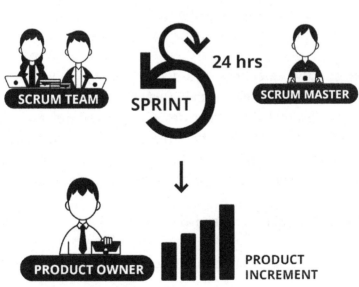

SCRUM TEAM

24 hrs

SPRINT

SCRUM MASTER

PRODUCT OWNER

PRODUCT INCREMENT

SCRUM MEETINGS:

Sprint planning meeting: This is the meeting where the work to be done in the next sprint is planned. During this meeting, the development team and the Product Owner establish the sprint objectives and the tasks necessary to achieve them.

Daily meeting: This is a meeting where the development team meets each day to give a brief update on the work that has been done since the last meeting, the work that will be done that day and if there are any obstacles that need to be resolved.

Demo meeting: This is the meeting in which the development team presents the work done during the sprint to the Product Owner and other interested parties. The objective is to get the go-ahead and thus make partial deliveries of the product and check that they meet the customer's expectations.

Retrospective meeting: This is a meeting in which the development team reflects on the way they worked in the sprint that has just ended and discusses what worked well and what could be improved in the future. The aim is to identify areas for improvement, not in terms of the product, but in terms of the team's work, and to establish an action plan for the next iteration.

When is SCRUM recommended?

This methodology is particularly recommended when:

- Deliveries do not correspond to what the customer requires.
- Customers change their requirements
- Deliveries take too long

- Costs soar
- Quality is not acceptable
- Reactivity to competition is needed
- Team morale is low and turnover is high.
- Inefficiencies need to be systematically identified and addressed.
- You want to work using a specialized process in the product development

In SCRUM, it is important that team members work collaboratively and that clear objectives are set for each sprint. It is also essential to maintain open and transparent communication, both during the sprint and at the review meeting. In addition, it is advisable to use digital tools for task management and for communication between team members.

In short, SCRUM is a highly effective agile methodology for project and team management. Its focus on collaboration, transparency and continuous improvement make it a valuable tool for any company or team seeking to increase efficiency and effectiveness in their work.

If you are interested in implementing SCRUM in your company or team, I recommend that you get proper training and that you have the collaboration of a committed team willing to learn and improve constantly.

KANBAN

It is based on visualizing work and limiting work in progress to optimize work flow. The methodology is divided into columns and cards representing project tasks, and focuses on continuously improving the work process.

Here are the key elements of KANBAN:

TO DO	IN PROGRESS	DONE
■□□□■ ■■■□□ □□□■■ ■■■■■ □□	■■■□■ □□■	□□□■■ ■■■

KANBAN Board: This is the main component of KANBAN. It is a board with columns representing the different stages of the work process and cards representing the tasks to be performed. The board should be visible to the whole team and should be updated regularly. Trello is an excellent platform to put this methodology into practice.

Work in progress limit: This is the maximum number of tasks that can be held in each column of the dashboard at any given time. Setting work in progress limits helps to avoid overload and to maintain a steady workflow.

Workflow: The set of steps that must be followed to complete a task, from request to final delivery. The workflow should be clear and represented in the columns of the dashboard.

Follow-up meetings: Although not mandatory, regular meetings are recommended to review the progress of the work. During these meetings the team discusses ongoing and upcoming tasks.

Advantages of using KANBAN:

- It allows you to visualize your work at a glance.
- It allows you to focus on the execution of tasks independently.
- Allows for multiple variations and evolution of your KANBAN adapting it to the needs of your company or team.
- It allows you to check progress on all your projects visually.

The key is to visualize the workflow and set work-in-progress limits for each task. It is also important to analyse bottlenecks and take steps to eliminate them. In this case, it is essential that the team is committed to the methodology and that regular meetings are held to discuss performance and make adjustments if necessary.

In summary, KANBAN is a highly effective agile project management methodology that focuses on visualizing work and optimizing work flow. Its focus on continuous improvement makes it a valuable tool for any company or team looking to increase the efficiency and effectiveness of their work.

If you are interested in implementing KANBAN in your company or team, I recommend that you are properly trained and that you have the collaboration of a committed team willing to constantly learn and improve.

KEY POINTS:

- SCRUM and KANBAN are two very effective agile methodologies for project and team management in a business environment.

- Both focus on collaboration, transparency and continuous improvement, and can be applied in any sector or business area.

- SCRUM is based on interaction and collaboration between team members, and is divided into *sprints* (interactions) of a fixed duration, typically 2-4 weeks.

- In SCRUM there are different roles and meetings that are fundamental for its correct implementation.

- KANBAN relies on job visualization and work-in-progress limitation to optimize the work flow.

- KANBAN uses columns and cards representing project tasks, and focuses on continuously improving the work process.

16

COLLABORATIVE WORK. TRELLO.

Collaborative working tools can help managers and middle managers and their teams to increase their productivity.

In today's world, and especially in teams in remote locations or teleworking, collaboration is even more essential for business success. There are many tools that can help foster teamwork and improve productivity.

Team communication platforms: Team communication platforms are essential for collaboration. These tools allow team members to communicate and collaborate in real time, regardless of their geographic location. The most popular tools are Slack, Microsoft Teams and Zoom.

Project management tools: Project management tools are essential to ensure that projects are completed on time and on budget. These tools allow for task assignment, progress tracking and deadline management. Popular options include Trello, Asana and Basecamp.

Document collaboration tools: Document collaboration tools are essential to ensure that team members can work together on documents in real time. These tools allow collaborative editing and commenting on documents, which can be useful in the creation of proposals, presentations and other materials. Popular tools include Google Docs, Microsoft Word and Dropbox Paper.

Cloud storage platforms: Cloud storage platforms allow team members to access files remotely from any location. This is especially useful for geographically distributed teams. Popular options include Dropbox, Google Drive and Microsoft's OneDrive.

Video conferencing tools: Video conferencing tools are essential for virtual collaboration. These tools allow online meetings with remote participants and can be an effective alternative to face-to-face meetings. Popular options include Zoom, Teams, Skype and Google Meets.

These collaborative work tools can be essential for increasing productivity. Team communication platforms, project management tools, document collaboration, cloud storage platforms and video conferencing tools can be valuable tools for improving collaboration and increasing productivity. So, don't hesitate to try some of these tools and see how they can help your team collaborate better and be more productive!

TRELLO

It is a project management and productivity tool that can be very useful for both personal management and team collaboration.

Before I continue, a clarification: I am not an expert in Trello, I am simply going to give you a few hints so that you can get to know this tool, which has great potential for applying many of the methodologies in this book, and which is relatively simple and accessible to everyone.

Personally, despite being an engineer, I do not consider myself a very "technological" person. I firmly believe that what really matters is not the tool but the use we make of it, as I mentioned at the beginning of this book.

However, when I discovered Trello in 2016, I found it so simple, flexible and intuitive that I decided to incorporate it into my "toolbox". Without a doubt, during all this time it has been a great ally for me.

You see, until then, my productivity had worked perfectly with my notebook to write down my to do list. But I didn't carry that notebook with me everywhere, whereas my mobile phone, most of the time, I did.

I also have to tell you that Trello can be as simple or as sophisticated as you want it to be. It can be used at both individual and team level.

If you don't know it yet, I recommend that you at least download the app on your mobile phone and start in the simplest way: a board with a couple of lists. Watch the tutorials and as you become more familiar you can add more possibilities.

Trello is a project management tool based on the use of cards and boards. Each card represents a task or activity, and can be moved between different columns representing the status of the task, such as *Inbox, To do list* and *On hold*. Dashboards can even be shared with other team members, enabling real-time collaboration and project tracking.

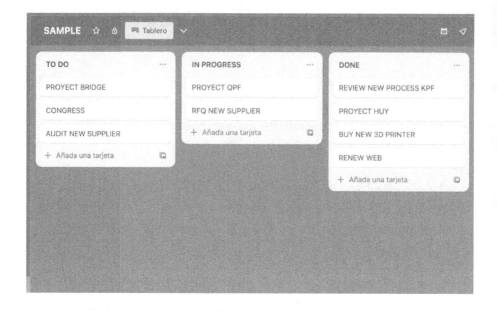

How can we apply Trello to improve our personal productivity?

First, we can use it as a daily or weekly to-do list, organizing our activities in different tabs and columns according to their priority or status. This allows us to clearly and easily visualize everything we have to do and when, avoiding forgetfulness and helping us to plan our time more effectively.

Personally, I find it very useful to have Trello on my mobile. If I'm out of the office and I remember something I need to do, I can just put it in my Trello and have the peace of mind that I'll manage it in a timely manner.

I also use it when I want to capture an image, or when I see a post on social media that I find interesting but don't have the time to read at that moment. I send it to Trello and when I am, for example, waiting to enter a meeting or in the doctor's waiting room, I look it up and read it calmly.

We can also use Trello to set long-term goals and projects, dividing them into different cards and setting deadlines and priorities for each one. In this way, we can keep an overview of our projects and make progress on them in an organized and structured way.

Trello and collaborative work

For use in teams, Trello is a very useful tool for collaboration and project management. Each team member can have his or her own task list and be responsible for their own progress, but they can also share cards and collaborate on more complex tasks or large- scale projects.

In addition, Trello integrates easily with other project management and productivity tools and methodologies. For example, we can use the Kanban methodology, which is based on the use of cards and columns for project management and task tracking. We can also integrate Trello with other project management tools for a more complete and effective management.

In short, Trello is a very versatile and adaptable tool that can be used both for personal management and for collaboration in work teams. Its intuitive and easy-to-use interface makes it a very accessible tool for any type of user, from beginners to the most advanced.

In short, if you want to improve your personal productivity or that of your team, I recommend you try Trello and discover for yourself all the advantages it can offer. You will see how using it can help you better organize your tasks, make progress on your projects and collaborate more effectively with other team members. Go ahead and give it a try!

KEY POINTS:

- Collaborative working tools can be essential to increase productivity and collaboration.

- The main ones are:
  - Team communication platforms
  - Project management tools
  - Collaboration on documents
  - Cloud storage platforms
  - Videoconferencing tools

- Trello:
  - Trello is an intuitive and accessible tool
  - It is flexible and a good support for many of the methodologies discussed here.
  - It can be used both individually and in teams.

17

PRODUCTIVITY OR PRESENTEEISM?

I remember when I started working in Ireland. I loved my job and I also wanted to make a good impression, so I stayed in the office more than my allotted hours.

Until one day one of my colleagues warned me to stop doing it. He told me that in Ireland and other northern European countries, if you work longer hours, you give the impression that you are not able to do your job in the hours you are supposed to work. Basically, he said, you give the image of being an unproductive person. That surprised me a lot, because in Spain and maybe in some other countries, spending long hours in the office was seen as a good thing.

After ten years of living and working in other countries, I realized that in Spain, not only is presenteeism encouraged, but it can also be mistaken for productivity. As a result, despite spending more hours at work, there is no increase in output.

A few months ago an employer complained that one of his employees always arrived and left on time. He never stayed longer than the official working hours. This in principle should not be the criterion for assessing performance, we would have to base it on the results that person achieves.

We can have people in our team who keep to their schedule and perform, but we can also have the opposite: people who spend more hours than anyone else in the office and fail to meet their targets.

What is the result of encouraging presenteeism?

If we evaluate our employees by the amount of time they spend in the office, without setting clearly defined goals, we run the risk that they will spend hours and hours at their jobs without being productive. Moreover, it has been shown that after a certain number of hours we are no longer productive, not to mention the imbalances that arise between family life and professional life.

Long hours in the office do not necessarily translate into productivity, but rather into:

- Cost of overtime
- Lack of family reconciliation
- Lack of motivation
- Lower productivity
- Fatigue
- Boredom

Do we penalize productivity?

How is productivity sometimes penalized? When someone leaves early because they have finished their work, they can be burdened with more tasks until they are burnt out.

This also happens at the team level, when they perceive that the result of performing better is perhaps not recognition, but the threat that there may be a surplus of people and that people may have to be laid off.

All this can make our team perceive that being productive can be counterproductive, i.e. something that can have negative consequences. A paradox I have seen on more than one occasion.

What are our options?
I think there is still a lot of work to be done in this direction, and that the solution lies in two keys:

- Clearly define the objectives and results to be achieved.
- Fostering self-responsibility and commitment within our teams.

It is clear that there are certain positions that require presence, such as those that offer a service to the public or establishments with business hours. But not all positions require the employee to be physically present at a location.

I am in favour of working by objectives, defining them clearly and using their achievement as a basis for evaluating the performance of our team members. If they decide to do it productively, the reward could be that they can leave the office earlier.

Set goals and let employees choose how to organize themselves to achieve them.

This will lead to more motivation and commitment than if they simply interpret their work as spending hours sitting in the office.

To begin to put it into practice, it would be necessary to take certain measures:

- Define objectives clearly.
- Flexibility of timetables.
- Follow-up on results.
- Rewarding productivity.
- Encourage commitment and self-responsibility.
- Good communication.

In short, the number of hours spent in the office does not necessarily translate into productivity. Let's set clear goals and encourage commitment and self-responsibility. Let's base our performance and that of our teams on the results that are achieved.

KEY POINTS:

- More hours in the office do not necessarily mean this should translate into higher productivity.

- Encouraging presenteeism can have negative consequences not only on productivity, but also on team motivation.

- It is important not to penalize productivity.

- Having clearly defined objectives, encouraging self-responsibility and good monitoring of results can give us more accurate data on the team's productivity.

18

TELEWORK AND PRODUCTIVITY

Since the pandemic passed through our lives, telework has come to most of us in one form or another. In many companies it was a one-off, while in others it is here to stay, in fully or partially.

It is clear that not everyone's home environment is the same: while some may prefer to work in the office, others clearly benefit more from teleworking.

In this chapter I want to talk about some practical tips that can help us be more productive while working from home.

Establish a routine: It is important to maintain a daily routine that allows you to work in an organized and effective way. Establish fixed times for starting and ending your workday, as well as for breaks and meals.

Create a suitable workspace: Dedicate a space in your home to work comfortably, without distractions and with the necessary resources. Make sure you have a good connection to the Internet and a comfortable chair that allows you to maintain a proper posture.

Set clear goals and objectives: Define clear goals and objectives for each day, week and month. This way you will have a guide that allows you to focus on what really matters and prioritize your tasks.

Use technology tools: Take advantage of available technology tools to improve communication, organization and task management. You can use video calling applications, project management platforms, chat and email tools, among others.

Communicate effectively: Communication is key in teleworking. Make sure you communicate effectively with your co-workers, customers and suppliers.

Avoid distractions: When teleworking, it is easy to get distracted by household chores or social media. To avoid this, set clear boundaries and avoid unnecessary distractions during your work day. You can apply the Pomodoro technique for this.

Take regular breaks: It is important to take regular breaks during your working day. Get up, walk around and stretch to avoid fatigue and muscle tension.

Take care of your eyes: Rest your eyes, if you spend a lot of time in front of the screen try to look out of the window at longer distances from time to time.

Maintain a healthy lifestyle: Teleworking can lead to a sedentary and unhealthy lifestyle. It is therefore important that you maintain a healthy lifestyle with a good diet and regular physical activity.

Set boundaries between work and personal life: It is important to set clear boundaries between work and personal life to avoid burnout and stress. Make time for yourself and your family outside working hours.

Be flexible and adaptable: In teleworking it is important to be flexible and adaptable to change. Make sure you keep abreast of developments and adapt to new circumstances to maintain productivity and well-being.

I hope you have found these tips useful. Remember, working from home can be challenging, but with the right attitude and the implementation of these practical tips, you can be more productive than ever.

KEY POINTS:

- Since the pandemic, teleworking has become much more common in companies.

- Take care of your well-being and your health.

- Certain guidelines can help us to telework in a more effective way. effectively, highlighting:
    - Working for results
    - Creating a good environment
    - Taking care of communication and communication tools collaborative work

19

STRESS AND PRODUCTIVITY

Being aware of the relationship between productivity and stress is crucial for leaders who want to optimize their performance. Although stress is sometimes thought of as simply a friend of productivity, the truth is that the relationship between these two concepts is much more complex.

It is important to understand that stress is a natural response of the body to situations of pressure or danger. In small ways, stress can even be useful and beneficial. For example, if we have a deadline for an important project, it is normal to feel a little stressed, but this can motivate us to work harder and be more productive in order to meet the deadline.

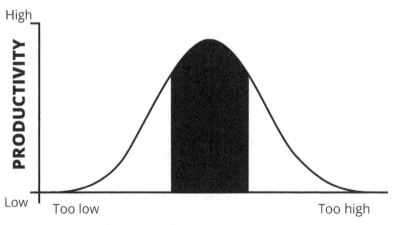

However, when the level of stress is too high or becomes chronic, i.e. when it is experienced over a prolonged period of time, it can have negative effects on health and productivity.

A high level of stress can block us and exhaust us, so that our productivity can be very negatively affected.

On the other hand, chronic stress can affect the quality of sleep, increase anxiety and depression, and decrease the ability to concentrate and remember.

It can also negatively affect motivation and creativity, which can make it more difficult to solve complex problems or think outside the box.

Here are some practical tips to apply in your day-to-day life to maintain good time management and reduce stress:

1. **Identify your daily priority tasks:** To do this you can use some of the methodologies I explain in this book: time quadrants and the Pareto method.

2. **Turn off notifications:** If you are already stressed, every time an alert sounds on your mobile or computer your stress level will increase. In addition, these interruptions will slow down your work and therefore make you even more stressed.

3. **GTD and Pomodoro:** These two methodologies will not only help you be more productive, but will also help you keep your stress level at bay. In addition, seeing that you

have your tasks under control and that you can execute them without interruption provides peace of mind.

4. **Set reasonable goals**: Set realistic objectives for yourself and your team. Remember the SMART format. Setting unattainable goals will only frustrate and stress you even more.

5. **Learn to delegate tasks:** To avoid overloading yourself with work and concentrate on what really matters. Remember the keys seen in this book to delegate properly so that it does not become another source of stress.

6. **Set realistic deadlines:** This way, you can avoid procrastination and stress in your tasks and projects. If necessary, break them down into sub-tasks to make them more manageable.

7. **Use productivity tools and technologies:** Such as time and task management applications or automation tools to reduce workload. Choose those that make your life easier and not the opposite. Sometimes overuse of technology or tools that are too complex can even make the situation worse.

8. **Learn to say "no":** Especially to tasks that are not a priority or are beyond your reach. Remember the guidelines we saw in this book.

9. **Take regular breaks:** To maintain energy and concentration. If you are one of those who forgets to rest, the Pomodoro method can help you here. It is also important to respect

your sleeping hours. Not getting enough sleep often takes its toll.

10. **Practice relaxation techniques** such as meditation and yoga, which not only reduce stress, but will teach you to recognise stress in your body and know when to stop before it's too late.

11. **Physical exercise:** Some people are not so keen on relaxation techniques and prefer something more active. Sport is a great way to unwind and generate the hormones that give us a feeling of well-being. Choose the form of physical exercise that best suits your tastes and possibilities. And if you enjoy it, all the better! Exercising not only takes care of your physical health, but also your mental health.

12. **Maintain a healthy and balanced diet:** This habit helps to maintain physical and mental health.

13. **Set clear boundaries between work and personal life:** Spend time doing activities you enjoy outside of work.

14. **Seek professional support**: If the stress is too much to handle on your own, you can seek counselling to improve the situation.

We also need to be aware that stress is contagious. A stressed leader will not only be less productive, but can also pass it on to his or her team and have the same negative effect on them. It is therefore worth paying attention to this issue.

KEY POINTS:

- While moderate levels of stress can optimize productivity, too much stress will have negative effects on performance.

- Good time management and the implementation of these practical tips can help reduce stress levels.

- Stress is contagious, and the leader's stress can affect his or her productivity and that of the rest of the team.

20

SHARPENING THE SAW

TO BE MORE PRODUCTIVE

In this chapter I want to talk about a very important topic that we often overlook: the importance of taking care of ourselves in order to be more productive in our work.

We often find ourselves in situations where the workload seems overwhelming and leaves us no time for anything else. However, it is crucial that we find ways to take care of ourselves and take time for ourselves if we want to be effective leaders and achieve high performance.

This is no more and no less than the seventh habit in Stephen Covey's book. A habit that is sometimes not given the importance it deserves and is even forgotten.

Before I continue, I would like to share a story that helps to better understand this concept:

Once upon a time, two woodcutters went into the forest to cut wood; one of them, a big, strong man, began to cut with great enthusiasm, without resting for a minute. The other, a little smaller, was also sawing. firewood, but unlike his companion, every now and then he stopped. At the end of the day, the first of them, who had stopped practically for nothing, looked up and saw that his companion's woodpile was considerably larger than his own. All indignant and perplexed, he went to him and said: "How can it be that you have cut more wood than me, if you have been stopping practically every hour? His companion replied, "Quite simply, because every time I stopped it was to sharpen my saw".

Many times we are so busy in our daily routine that we don't stop to "sharpen the saw", without realizing that it is an investment of our time in something that will make us more productive in the end.

On the other hand, we have to take care of our body, probably the most important tool we have. To do this, it is important to take care of our diet, sleep and regular exercise. In short, to take care of ourselves. Our body has to last us a lifetime.

When we take care of our bodies we improve our health and energy levels. In addition, if we look good physically, it can increase our self-esteem and self-confidence. This will affect our performance and the energy we radiate positively.

As a leader, you are sharpening your saw right now by reading this book. You are cultivating your knowledge and skills to improve your productivity, which will help you perform better in your day-to-day life.

How can you apply this concept in your daily life? Our mind and body are the best and most important tools at our disposal. It is important that both are in good shape to face difficulties and challenges.

Here are some practical tips:

1. **Exercise:** It will keep you active and fitter, healthier and more energetic to face new challenges. It will also help you keep stress levels at bay.

2. **Educate yourself:** Never stop learning, there is always something to improve. Besides being a way to sharpen your saw, learning something new can also be a great way to broaden your skills and perspectives and help you increase your productivity.

3. **Read books that inspire you:** Apart from providing learning, books can also inspire and motivate us to achieve our goals. Especially if you put those learnings into practice. I recommend that every time you read a book (or take a course) you make a summary of the main learnings and make an action plan to put them into practice. If you don't have time to read, another option is to listen to audiobooks or podcasts while driving, playing sports, walking or any other waiting time.

4. **Take care of your body:** Our body is one of the most important tools at our disposal. The more we look after it, the more productive we will be. How can you achieve this? In addition to exercise, take care of your diet, sleep and rest. There is a body-mind connection. Both play a key role in our performance and productivity.

5. **Take care of your mind:** Keeping a learner's mindset, training and reading will help you to have an active mind. In addition, we can add practices such as meditation and *mindfulness*. These disciplines are increasingly present in the business world. They have been scientifically proven to have positive effects on our ability to concentrate, and even on the prevention of stress and depression, which translates into increased performance and productivity.

6. **Make a list of activities that help you recharge**: reading, listening to music, cooking or just spending time outdoors. Once you have your list, be sure to schedule time for these activities in your weekly calendar.

Remember that taking care of yourself is not a selfish activity, but rather a way to ensure that you are at your best to lead your team and achieve success in your work. So take the time to sharpen your saw and take care of yourself, and you will see your productivity and effectiveness at work increase.

Set aside time in your schedule for things that h e l p you take care of yourself and be more productive. We tend to downplay it and let other issues hijack our attention, time and energy.

Setting aside time in our schedule for activities that keep us physically and mentally fit is crucial for our productivity.

This does not mean that we cannot have some flexibility. An example: Imagine you decide to set aside every Monday, Wednesday and Friday from 20:00 to 21:00 for exercise, and one day you have a business trip or other unforeseen circumstances. You can decide to move that exercise time to a Tuesday or Thursday, or to a different time of the day. In other words: you find another time, but you don't erase it from your schedule. Whereas if we don't make sure we reserve these slots in the calendar, we will always find a reason to keep postponing it indefinitely, and that's the best way to make sure we never do it.

EXAMPLE OF "SHARPENING THE SAW":

In my most stressful time, when I moved to the Netherlands with my new position and a team under my charge for the first time, I had no time for anything, and yet that was when I most needed to "sharpen the saw". It was then that I discovered the book that I mention so often in my publications, conferences and workshops, *The 7 Habits of Highly Effective People* by S. Covey. Well, my way of "reading" this great book was to take it in audiobook format in my car, and every time I drove I listened to Steven Covey himself narrating his wise advice. I listened to it over and over again until it stuck in my memory. If you don't have time to read, incorporate audiobooks and personal development podcasts while doing other activities. It's a good way to get more out of your time and make time in your schedule for "sharpening the saw"

There are currently a large number of options for listening to content while travelling, playing sports, etc. In particular, the podcast format is becoming very popular.

Believe me, "sharpening the saw" is a great investment. You will have to put in some time, but you will reap great benefits, such as increased productivity and health, both physically and mentally.

When was the last time you stopped to "sharpen the saw"?

At company level it is also necessary to "sharpen the saw". Training our teams, working on leadership, encouraging teamwork and, in short, taking care of all those aspects that can make the difference between achieving high performance or not.

KEY POINTS:

- To sharpen the saw is to take care of our best tool - our body and mind - to be more productive.

- It is an investment that will result in a greater productivity.

- It is important to set aside time to do this.

- Your team also needs to sharpen the saw to be more productive.

21

DISCONNECT TO CONNECT

Sometimes we find ourselves in a situation where we cannot make progress on a task, no matter how hard we try. It may be that we are tired, blocked, or just can't find a way to solve a problem. And when that happens, many people are tempted to force their brain to keep working, but in reality that is often not the most efficient thing to do.

The truth is that when we are blocked, the best thing we can do is to switch off and walk away from the task at hand. This may seem like a waste of time, but it is actually an investment in our future productivity. When we take a break, we allow our brains to relax and process information more effectively. In addition, by stepping away from the task, we often find new perspectives and approaches that we had not considered before.

Haven't you ever had the feeling that sometimes you're thinking about something and can't come up with a solution, until just when you're doing something relaxing or relaxed, you suddenly have a brilliant idea? It happens to me often, especially on my walks in nature or when I'm exercising. Other times even when I wake up in the middle of the night. We can enhance our creativity through relaxation.

Trigger your eureka moment

The concept of the "eureka moment" goes back to the story of the Greek mathematician Archimedes, who lived in the third century B.C. According to legend, King Hieron II of Syracuse had commissioned Archimedes to determine whether a crown he had acquired was pure gold or had been adulterated with other, less valuable metals. Archimedes was struggling with the problem, until one day while in his bath, he noticed that the water level rose when he immersed himself in the bath. This observation led him to understand the principle of the law of buoyancy and suddenly he had a eureka moment when he realised how he could solve the dilemma of the crown. According to legend, Archimedes ran naked through the streets shouting "Eureka!" (I've found it!) to celebrate his discovery.

Of course, it is not a question of taking an indefinite break. The ideal is to set a set time to switch off, whether it is half an hour, an hour or even a whole day if necessary. During that time, do something that relaxes you and makes you feel good. It could be reading a book, going for a walk, exercising, meditating or just sitting and doing nothing.

Once you've disconnected and rested, it's time to reconnect, but not just any old way. Instead of simply picking up where you left off, try to focus on different options or perspectives that you have considered during your time of disconnection. Perhaps you have found a new source of inspiration, perhaps someone has given you a new idea or you have had an insight while meditating.

In short, disconnecting when we are blocked is an effective strategy to improve our productivity and do our work more efficiently. So don't hesitate: if you feel blocked, give yourself a break, reconnect with new perspectives and go for it!

Another eureka moment in history: Newton and the apple.

The story of the apple falling on Isaac Newton's head is one of the best-known anecdotes in the history of science, and is often cited as an example of the eureka moment. According to legend, in the autumn of 1666, while Newton was resting under an apple tree, an apple fell on his head, leading him to wonder why the apple always fell downwards and not upwards. This simple question was the starting point for his investigations into the law of gravity.

Newton's eureka moment was not as sudden as legend suggests. He had been pondering the problems of physics for years and had been working on the law of gravity in the years leading up to his eureka moment. However, the story of the apple is a perfect example of how a seemingly serendipitous or trivial discovery can lead to a brilliant idea that changes the course of history. Newton's eureka moment was the result of years of work and reflection, but the apple incident was the catalyst that led to his final understanding of the law of gravity.

THE 7 DIMENSIONS OF REST

Some time ago I came across an interesting article by Saundra Dalton-Smith. I initially shared it online with a brief translation, but given the interest it aroused, I have decided to include my own version of it in this book.

We live in a fast-paced society where we continually strive for high performance, and where we are reaching a level of fatigue, stress and **burnout** *that is becoming chronic.*

Have you ever had a continuous lack of energy that you couldn't recover despite trying to get more sleep? It is clear that a good sleep routine is essential, not only for the rest of the body, but also for the resetting of the mind. But sometimes it may not be enough.

Without adequate rest we cannot optimize our productivity.

We need to include the different types of rest in order to achieve not only higher performance, but also productivity that is sustainable over time and does not take its toll on our health.

Saundra Dalton explains it by saying that there are actually at least 7 types of rest that we need.

Physical rest: Which can be in turn:
> **Passive**: This would consist mainly of what is understood as the traditional concept of rest, such as sleeping, napping, resting, etc.
> **Active**: With restorative activities such as yoga, stretching or massages to help improve circulation and body flexibility - sometimes even a good workout can leave you feeling like new!

Mental rest: Sometimes we want to overcome our dullness with large quantities of coffee, but all we achieve is to become more irritable and stressed. We find it hard to switch off even when we are no longer at work or when it is time to sleep. Our mind needs to switch off. To do so, it is not essential to go on holiday; we can achieve this in our day-to-day life by taking short breaks or disconnections throughout our day, for example, every 2 hours.

In my particular case, whenever my schedule allows it, I always include a short walk mid-morning that helps me to disconnect and resume my activity with a fresher and clearer mind. Often 10 minutes is enough.

It is also good to have a notebook to write down those ideas that come to you at night when you are trying to sleep, once you write them down it will be easier for them to stop running around in your head and you will be able to fall asleep.

Sensory rest: Away from screens, blue light and noise, whether we are in the office or teleworking. When we spend hours and hours in front of the screen and with external noise, our senses are overloaded.

To do this, we can focus our breaks on closing our eyes or switching off our devices, silencing unnecessary alarms and notifications.

The walk I was talking about earlier is also good for our eyes. Staring at a close-up screen all the time, especially when many of us have spent two years doing a large part of our work online, is fatal for our eyes, which need to focus far away. A short walk not only gives us a break from screens, but also allows us to focus our gaze at longer distances.

Creative rest: Especially important for those who need to generate ideas to solve problems. There are jobs that need this creativity to achieve better results. Spending time in nature, especially in beautiful natural surroundings, is recommended for this type of break. Another source of creativity is to surround yourself with art: you can include images in your work environment that inspire you and make your space more welcoming and creative. You are hardly going to be inspired by spending 40 hours a week between four dull and monotonous walls.

Emotional rest: Sometimes, it's the emotional aspect that becomes overwhelming and drains all our energy. Being able to free ourselves from negative emotions and recharge with positive ones is necessary to feel active and energetic. There are increasing studies linking emotions not only to our mental well-being but also to physical health.

Being able to express how we feel, so that when someone asks us, 'How are you?' we can openly say, 'I'm not doing well,' and being able to externalize our emotions is a way to prevent or alleviate emotional exhaustion. Even resorting to assertively saying 'no' when appropriate is essential to avoid reaching this type of exhaustion.

Social rest: This type of rest can be closely linked to the previous one. In our environment there may be people who exhaust us emotionally and others who make us feel good and fill us with energy.

How can we achieve this kind of rest? By avoiding toxic people and surrounding ourselves with vitamin people. And the good news is that this can even work *online*. Fortunately, though, those essential, battery-charging meetings and hugs that have been sorely missed in the worst months of the pandemic are already back.

Spiritual rest: We have the capacity to go beyond the physical and mental, either through meditation or by finding purpose and meaning in our lives. Having a "what for", giving meaning to what we do, can make us better able to endure difficult times. Viktor Frankl already saw this in the Nazi concentration camps, and reflected on it in his book *Man's Search for Meaning*.

One final word of warning: Fatigue can also be a symptom of a major medical condition, so if you think you might be suffering from fatigue, consult your doctor.

If you want to see Saundra Dalton-Smith's TED talk, you can find it on YouTube.

And now that you know all this, what are you going to include in your daily routine to improve your rest?

KEY POINTS:

- It is important to disconnect in order to reconnect.

- Eureka moments are the result of the disconnection and relaxation.

- There are different ways to increase our productivity through rest.

- We need seven types of rest: physical, mental, sensory, creative, emotional, social and spiritual.

22

LET'S GET TO WORK

I hope that you have already started to put the learnings from this book into practice. I recommend that you start with the activity log, it will give you a more objective view of how you use your time and will help you to make a good diagnosis. You can't improve if you don't know where you need to focus.

I suggest that after exploring all these methodologies, you adapt and combine them as you see fit, according to your tastes, your work and your lifestyle.

Remember: it's not the tool, it's how you use it.

The goal here is for you to take control of your time and not the other way around. Being in control will not only lead to better results, it will also give you greater peace of mind and keep your stress levels in check.

I also invite you to connect with me on LinkedIn, to follow my publications and *Newsletter* where you will see that I publish topics of interest to managers and middle managers with teams in charge (or aspiring to be).

It's not what you learn,
is what you do with what you learn.

ABOUT INMA RÍOS

Inma Ríos is an expert in Leadership Development and High-Performance Teams, an engineer from the Polytechnic University of Valencia. International speaker. Author of several leadership books Top Women Leaders 2022 Award.

Inma has managed Supply Chain departments at EMEA level (Europe, Middle East and Africa), managing suppliers, production and multidisciplinary and multicultural teams. She has **25 years of professional experience in multinationals in various European countries**

Inma has first-hand experience of leading teams in complex and challenging environments. She knows how it feels to be under pressure and how to stay motivated, as well as how to achieve positive results in difficult situations. That is why her approach is based on **practical and effective solutions** that can be implemented in any team's day-to-day work.

Since 2013 she has been a consultant and trainer for organizations and business schools. She has helped more than 100 companies to develop high-performance teams and has trained thousands of managers to develop the mindset and skills of great leaders in order to achieve more motivated and productive teams. She has more than 5000 students from all over the world in her online video courses. Her podcast ¡ENTRENA TU LIDERAZGO! is listened to in more than 30 countries.

Her most relevant qualifications include: Professor of several MBA programmes at FBS Fundesem Business School, teacher and consultant accredited by the School of Industrial Organization. Master's Degree in *Coaching* with NLP and Emotional Intelligence accredited by ICF (International Coach Federation). Professional Coach certified by ASESCO (Spanish *Coaching Association*), Systemic Team *Coaching* by the Academy of Executive Coaching in London. Certified Behavioral and Motivational Analyst by TTI Talent Insights. Scrum Master. Certified Agile Team Facilitator by IC Agile (ICP- ATF) in the UK.

You can access Inma´s website, social networks, books, video, courses, etc. in this QR.

OTHER BOOKS BY INMA RÍOS

KEYS TO SUCCESSFUL LEADERSHIP
(SOON AVAILABLE IN ENGLISH!!)

Have you just been promoted to a position of greater responsibility? Do you aspire to become a great leader?

The purpose of this book is to provide these professionals who suddenly find themselves in a new situation (a team in charge, increased responsibilities, new roles, etc.) with a guide to help them achieve better results.

OTHER BOOKS BY LYNN A. RICE

EQUIPOS
MOTIVADOS
EQUIPOS
PRODUCTIVOS

MANUAL PRÁCTICO
PARA DIRECTIVOS

INMA RÍOS

Prólogo de Juanma Romero,
director de "Emprende" en RTVE

Editorial
Tébar Flores

MOTIVATED TEAMS, PRODUCTIVE TEAMS
(SOON AVAILABLE IN ENGLISH!!)

Do you have a team in your charge? Do you want to learn about methodologies that will help you in your day-to-day work?

A High Performance Team is a team that achieves great results and whose members are motivated and committed. Financial reward is not the only way to motivate a team. More often than not, what really motivates them is having clearly defined objectives, a healthy and motivating leadership, the feeling of being an essential part of the organization and that the work done is valued and considered necessary.

What are you waiting for to hone your leadership skills?

MORE RESOURCES AND SOCIAL NETWORKS

If you liked this book and are interested in following my content in the future, here are some options:

***Newsletter* on LinkedIn:** Where I publish a weekly article that will be sent to you as soon as you subscribe.

I invite you to visit **my website www.inmarios.com** and to subscribe to my mailing list. You will receive first-hand information about new books, courses, special promotions and other interesting topics.

Listen to my **podcast** *¡ENTRENA TU LIDERAZGO!* (at the moment only available in Spanish) where you can listen to my content while driving, exercising or doing other things. What better way to use your time to "sharpen your saw"? You can find it on various platforms: Spotify, Google Podcasts, Apple Podcast, Anchor, Ivoox, Breaker, Pocket Cast, Radio Public...

Social media. I invite you to share your inspiration by posting that phrase or whatever has caught your attention from this book on social networks and to tag me so that it reaches me, so I can greet you with a message.

- LinkedIn (www.linkedin.com/in/inmarios/)
- Instagram (@inmarios_)
- Twitter (@inmarios_)
- YouTube (www.youtube.com/c/INMARIOS)
- Facebook (@InmaRiosFB)

You can access my website, social networks, my books, video courses, etc. in this QR.

PROFESSIONAL SERVICES

OF INMA RÍOS

I work mainly *in-company* with **management teams and middle management** to develop healthy and motivating leadership by training them in practical tools that help tremendously in the management of their teams. This is possible both in group and individual format.

I also guide companies and their leaders in the **Development of High Performance Teams,** making a diagnosis of their teams in order to get to know them better and identify strengths and areas for improvement. In my workshops, everyone participates actively and dynamically, leading to greater commitment and motivation, thus improving results.

The following options are available for:

- **LEADERSHIP DEVELOPMENT:** For managers and middle managers who wish to develop healthy and motivating leadership, training them in practical tools that help tremendously in the management of their teams. Group or individual modality can be chosen.

- **DEVELOPING HIGH-PERFORMANCE TEAMS:** By diagnosing your teams in order to get to know them better and to identify strengths and areas for improvement. Advice is given on the definition of objectives and the co-creation of action plans together with their collaborators. This takes place in workshops where everyone participates actively and dynamically, leading to a greater commitment to achieving these goals and, therefore, greatly improving results and motivation.

- **IN COMPANY TRAINING:** Can be chosen from a menu of workshops or customized according to the needs of each team: leadership, time management, assertive communication, etc.

- **ONLINE TRAINING:** Can be chosen from the menu of workshops or customized according to the needs of each team: leadership, time management, assertive communication, etc.

- **INTERNATIONAL SPEAKER:** Dynamic, agile conferences and talks with valuable content, including anecdotes and personal experiences to inspire with freshness in company events and other organizations.

Do you need more information?
I invite you to visit my website
www.inmarios.com.

BIBLIOGRAPHY

- Alcántara Gómez, A. (2015). *#SuperProfesional: tómate tu vida profesional como algo personal.*
- Allen, D. (2011). *Organízate con eficacia.*
- Allen, D. (2015). *Getting Things Done: The Art of Stress-free Productivity.*
- Altman, H. (2019). *KANBAN: Guía ágil paso a paso diseñada para ayudar a los equipos a trabajar juntos de manera más eficiente.*
- Blanchard, K., Zirgami, P., y Zirgami, D. (2000). *Leadership and the One Minute Manager.*
- Cirillo, Francesco (2018) *The Pomodoro Technique: The Life-Changing Time-Management.*
- Covey, S. R. (1989). *The 7 Habits of Highly Effective People* (Ed. revisada).
- Covey, S. R., (2013). *El octavo hábito.*
- Galindo, L., (2014). *Reilusionarse* (10ª ed.).
- Gebelein, S. H., Nelson-Neuhaus, C. J., Skube, C. J., Stevens, L. A., Hellervick, L. W., y Davis, B. L., (2010). *Successful Manager's Handbook* (8ª ed.).
- Goleman, D. (1996). *Inteligencia emocional.*
- Goleman, D. (2018). *Inteligencia emocional en la empresa (Imprescindibles).*
- Goleman, D. (2019). *Liderazgo. El poder de la inteligencia emocional.*
- Harvard Business Review (2015). *Performance Reviews.*

- Hawkings, P. (2011). *Leadership Team Coaching: Developing Collective Transformational Leadership.* Londres, Reino Unido: Kogan Page.
- Heller, R. (1997). *How to Delegate (Essential Managers Series).*
- Hicks, J. (2019). «New Research Shows Managers Are at an Increased Risk of Stress and Burnout — Here's How to Fight Back». *Thrive Global.* Recuperado de https://thriveglobal.com/stories/managers-management-challenges-avoid-stress-burnout.
- Lasa Gómez, C., Álvarez García, A., y De las Heras del Dedo, R. (2017). *Métodos ágiles. Scrum, Kanban, Lean (Manuales Imprescindibles).*
- Lombardo, M. M., y Eichinger, R. W. (2004). *FYI: For Your Improvement, A Guide for Development and Coaching* (4ª ed.).
- López, Á. (2017). *Cliente digital, vendedor digital: conoce las claves del social selling.*
- Martel, A. (2014). *Gestión práctica de proyectos con Scrum: desarrollo de software ágil para el Scrum Master.*
- Maurer, R. (2015). *Un pequeño paso puede cambiar tu vida: el método Kaizen.*
- Medline Plus. «Dormir bien». Recuperado de https://medlineplus.gov/spanish/healthysleep.html.
- Miralles, F., García, H. (2017). *El método Ikigai: despierta tu verdadera pasión y cumple tus propósitos vitales.*
- Nir, M., y Berniz, A. (2014). *Coaching y liderazgo: liderando equipos altamente efectivos - Guía práctica de coaching de equipos de alto rendimiento.*
- Ríos, C. (2019). *Come comida real: una guía para transformar tu alimentación y tu salud (Divulgación).*
- Ríos, I. (2018). *Equipos motivados, equipos productivos.*
- Ríos, I. (2020). *Claves para liderar con éxito.*

- Romero Martín, J. M., y Romero Nieva, J. (2019). *Lidera tu empresa en la cuarta revolución.*
- Sánchez, A. (2016). *Mi dieta cojea: Los mitos sobre nutrición que te han hecho creer (Divulgación).*
- Samsó, R. (2019). *El poder de la disciplina: el hábito que cambiará tu vida.*
- Spencer, L. M. (1993). *Competence At Work: Models for Superior Performance.*
- Thornton, C. (2016). *Group and Team Coaching: The secret life of groups.*
- Tonhauser, P. (2016). *Design Thinking Workshop: The 12 Indispensable Elements for a Design.*
- Villa, I. (2011). *Saber que se puede, veinte años después.* (Edición ampliada y actualizada).
- VV. AA. (2016). *El principio de Pareto: optimice su negocio con la regla del 80/20.*
- Walsh, P. (2014). «5 Ways To Save Your Middle Managers From Burnout». *FastCompany.* Recuperado de https://www.fastcompany.com/3028674/5-ways-to-save-your-middle-managers-from-burnout.
- Whitmore, J. (2018). *Coaching: el método para mejorar el rendimiento de las personas (Empresa).* Wolfe, I. (2004). *Understanding Business Values and Motivators.*

WEBGRAPHY

- https://jordisanchez.info/que-es-gtd
- https://superrhheroes.sesametime.com/que-es-el-metodo-gtd
- https://luisolavea.xyz/que-es-gtd
- https://sebastianpendino.com/gtd-getting-things-done
- https://sebastianpendino.com/aumentar-productividad-gtd-principios
- http://www.mytimemanagement.com/pareto-principle.html
- https://www.businessballs.com/self-management/paretos-80-20-rule-theory
- https://www.inspiringleadershipnow.com/how-to-use-the-pareto-principle-80-20-rule
- Diario de Navarra. Edición Digital (2016). «Una empresa con trabajadores felices puede aumentar su productividad hasta un 31 %». Recuperado de http://www.diariodenavarra.es/noticias/negocios/dn_management/contenidos/2016/11/15/una_empresa_con_trabajadores_felices_puede_aumentar_productividad_31_499012_2542.html.
- Diario Expansión. Edición Digital (2019). «Estar quemado ya es una enfermedad, "oficialmente"». Recuperado de https://www.expansion.com/sociedad/2019/07/03/5d1c6c3b468aebbe568b4612.html

- Retos Directivos. (2017). «*¿Empresas felices = empresas productivas?*». Recuperado de https://retos-directivos.eae.es/empresas-felices-empresasproductivas
- Fundació factor humà. (2016). «Herramientas de autoconocimiento en el ámbito laboral». Recuperado de https://factorhuma.org/attachments/article/12359/eines_autoconeixement_cast.pdf
- Augustine, A.: «How to Deal With Burnout as a Manager». *Themuse*. Recuperado de https://www.themuse.com/advice/how-to-deal-with-burnout-as-a-manager
- Blatto, L. E. (2012): «6 consejos para reconocer la labor del trabajador». *Gestiopolis*. Recuperado de https://www.gestiopolis.com/6-consejos-reconocer-labor-del-trabajador.
- https://ideas.ted.com/the-7-types-of-rest-that-every-person-needs/amp/

Made in the USA
Las Vegas, NV
21 April 2024

88974308R00095